Preparation Book for the
TOEFL Primary® Speaking

Contents

Introduction to the TOEFL® Young Students Series 4

About Preparation Book for the TOEFL Primary® Speaking ... 10

How to Use This Book 11

Characters 14

Unit 1 House ·· 15

Unit 2 Vacation ··· 31

Unit 3 Lunch Break! ·· 47

Unit 4 Field Trip ··· 63

Unit 5 Shopping Mall ·· 79

Unit 6 Science Class ··· 95

Actual Test 1 ·· 111

Actual Test 2 ·· 123

Answer Key ··· 별책

Introduction to the TOEFL® Young Students Series

About the TOEFL® Young Students Series (TOEFL YSS)

TOEFL YSS는 학생들의 학습 수준과 연령에 맞게 미국 ETS(Educational Testing Service)에서 개발한 시험으로, 학생들의 영어실력 측정 뿐만 아니라 다음 단계의 영어학습 지도에 대한 가이드를 제시합니다.
또한 영어에 대한 자신감은 물론 나아가서는 미래의 잠재력까지 키울 수 있도록 도움을 줄 수 있습니다.

TOEFL YSS Line-Up

Introduction to the TOEFL Primary® Tests

About TOEFL Primary®

TOEFL Primary®는 영어학습 입문 단계의 글로벌 영어 인증 시험으로 영어를 모국어로 사용하지 않는 나라의 어린 학습자들을 대상으로 전반적인 영어 능력을 측정합니다.

TOEFL Primary®는 PBT(Paper Based Tests) 방식의 TOEFL Primary® Reading and Listening Test – Step1 & Step2와 IBT(Internet Based Tests)방식의 TOEFL Primary® Speaking Test가 있습니다.

Test Options

시험 레벨	권장 대상	특징
TOEFL Primary® Step 1	초등생	영어를 시작하는 단계의 학생을 대상으로 익숙한 환경 및 주제(학교, 가정, 친구 등)로 구성된 내용을 통해 Reading & Listening 능력 평가
TOEFL Primary® Step 2	초등 고학년 ~ 중등 1학년	영어로 어느 정도 의사소통을 할 수 있는 학생을 대상으로 일상 생활의 범위를 넘어선 주제와 관련된 짧은 스토리와 대화 내용을 통해 Reading & Listening 능력 평가
TOEFL Primary® Speaking	초등생 ~ 중학생	다양한 레벨의 어린 학생들을 대상으로 IBT로 진행되며 일상 생활에서 필요한 영어 의사소통 능력 평가

Test Structure

– TOEFL Primary® Reading and Listening Test – Step 1

영역	문항 수	샘플 문항 수	총 문항 수	시험 시간	점수	등급
Reading	36	3	39	30분	100~109	1~4 등급 (☆로 표시)
Listening	36	5	41	30분	100~109	
Total	72	8	80	60분	200~218	

– TOEFL Primary® Reading and Listening Test – Step 2

영역	문항 수	샘플 문항 수	총 문항 수	시험 시간	점수	등급
Reading	36	1	37	30분	100~115	1~5 등급 (🏅로 표시)
Listening	36	3	39	35분	100~115	
Total	72	4	76	65분	200~230	

– TOEFL Primary® Speaking Test

영역	문항 수	시험 시간	점수	등급
Speaking	7~10	20분	1~27	1~5 등급 (🏅로 표시)

※ 공식 웹사이트: www.toeflyss.or.kr (리스닝 음원 및 학습용 자료 무료 다운로드)
  – 리스닝(Sample Answer) mp3 파일
  – Speaking 문제 유형 확인
  – 학습용 자료(단어 리스트 등)

■ Test Section – TOEFL Primary® Speaking Test

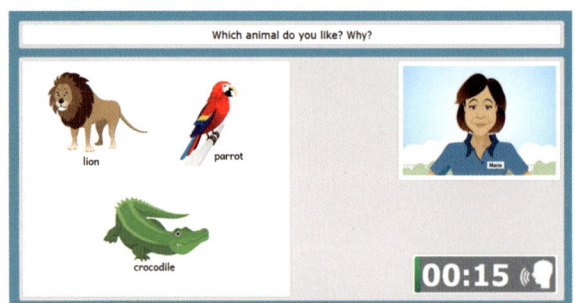

의견 표현/묘사
사진 몇 장을 보여주고 응시자가 하나를 선택한 후 사진에 대한 생각이나 의견을 말해야 합니다.
(응답시간 : 10~15초)

요청
서술자가 응시자에게 이야기에서 나오는 캐릭터에게 요청을 하라고 지시합니다.
(응답시간 : 5~15초)

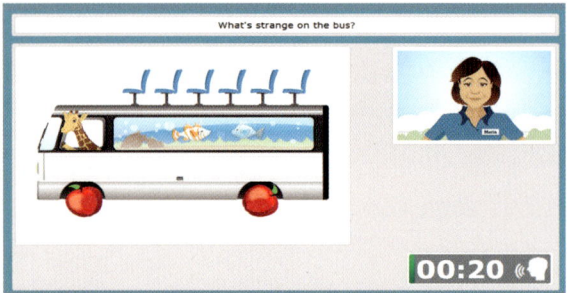

그림 설명
사진을 본 후 사진에서 이상하게 보이는 것들을 설명해야 합니다.
(응답시간 : 20초)

질문
서술자가 그림을 보여주면 응시자는 그림에 대한 3가지 질문을 해야 합니다.
(응답시간 : 30초)

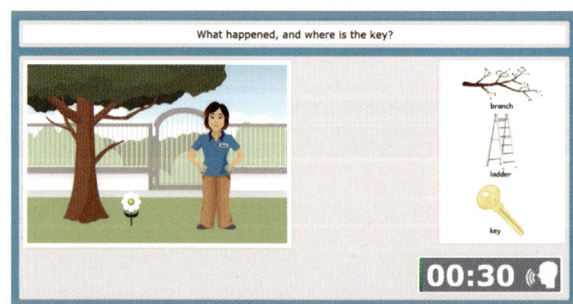

지시/안내
영상이나 사진들을 통해 캐릭터가 활동하는 모습을 보여주면 응시자는 캐릭터가 영상에서 보인 행동을 어떻게 진행했는지 설명해야 합니다.
(응답시간 : 30초)

서술
영상이나 사진을 확인하고 그 내용을 바탕으로 이야기를 만들어야 합니다.
(응답시간 : 30초)

Test Score Guide – TOEFL Primary® Speaking Test

Speaking Level — Typical students at this level:	Score	CEFR
🎖🎖🎖🎖🎖 영어로 서술을 확장하고, 여러 단계의 지시로 소통하며 이야기를 효과적으로 말합니다.	27	B2
	26	B2
	25	B1
	24	B1
	23	B1
	22	B1
🎖🎖🎖🎖 영어로 좋아하는 것을 표현, 설명하고 지시합니다.	21	A2
	20	A2
	19	A2
	18	A2
🎖🎖🎖 영어로 그들이 좋아하는 것을 말하고 어느 정도 지시를 합니다.	17	A1
	16	A1
	15	A1
	14	A1
	13	A1
	12	A1
	11	A1
	10	A1
🎖🎖 영어로 단어들과 간단한 문장을 사용해 말하기 시작합니다.	9	Below A1
	8	Below A1
	7	Below A1
	6	Below A1
	5	Below A1
🎖 영어로 단어와 간단한 구문들을 사용해 이야기하기를 시도합니다.	4	Below A1
	3	Below A1
	2	Below A1
	1	Below A1
이 학생들은 시험에 응답하지 않았거나 영어로 대답하지 않았습니다.	0	Not Applicable (NA)

- 점수는 0점에서 27점 사이이며(0~27) 각 레벨은 리본 개수로 표시됩니다.
- 리본 개수에 따른 영어 실력 설명과 다음 단계를 위한 추천 영어 학습법이 각 단계별로 제공되고 있습니다.
- 설명서에 나온 리본 개수에 따른 영어 실력 설명과 다음 단계를 위한 추천 영어 공부 방법은 각 레벨에 맞추어져 있으며, 모든 학생들을 위한 방법이 아닙니다.
- 각 레벨의 학생들은 자신 보다 낮은 레벨의 학생들이 갖춘 영어 실력을 갖추고 있다는 뜻도 됩니다.
- 시험 점수는 성적표의 하단에 나와 있으며 성적표를 보면 해당 학생의 레벨과 영어 실력을 알 수 있습니다.

레벨	영어 실력	다음 단계
🎖🎖🎖🎖🎖 5개중 5개의 리본	이 레벨의 학생은 영어로 서술을 확장하고, 여러 단계의 지시로 소통하며 이야기를 효과적으로 말합니다. 또한 성공적으로 질문하고 간단한 요청을 합니다. 이 학생은 다음과 같은 것을 할 수 있습니다: – 다양한 어휘와 문법적 구성을 효과적으로 사용 – 서술을 확장, 지시 그리고 이야기를 말하기 위한 적절한 세부사항을 포함 – 이해하기 쉬운 지시와 이야기를 만들 수 있도록 단어들과 구문들을 연결하는 것과 같은 문장 구조를 포함 – 질문과 요청을 적절히 하고 의미를 전달하기 위해 억양을 사용 – 발음 혹은 억양에 거의 문제없이 유창하게 말함	실력을 향상시키기 위해서 이 레벨의 학생은: – 나이에 맞는 학술적 내용을 읽고 듣는 연습을 합니다. – 나이에 맞는 학술적 내용에 대해 말하고 쓰는 연습을 합니다. – 학생의 영어 실력에 대해 좀 더 많은 정보를 얻기 위해 TOEFL Junior® Speaking 시험 응시를 고려합니다.
🎖🎖🎖🎖 5개중 4개의 리본	이 레벨의 학생은 간단한 이야기들이나 자신의 나이에 맞는 학술적 글을 읽고 이해합니다. 이 학생은 다음과 같은 것을 할 수 있습니다: – 적절한 단어 선택 사용 – 생각을 전달하기 위해 완전한 문장을 사용 – 적절한 문법 구조 사용 – 문의와 요청 문장을 만들기 시작 – 발음과 억양에 거의 문제없이 정확히 말함	실력을 향상시키기 위해서 이 레벨의 학생은: – 익숙한 장소, 물건, 사람들을 묘사하는 일상적이지 않은 단어들을 학습합니다. – 일상 생활과 관련된 주제들에 대해서 묻고 답하기를 연습합니다. – 학생이 읽는 이야기 그리고 보는 프로그램에서 장소, 인물 그리고 사건들에 대한 세부 사항 말하는 것을 연습합니다.
🎖🎖🎖 5개중 3개의 리본	이 레벨의 학생은 단순한 이야기를 이해할 수 있으며 자신의 나이에 맞는 학술적 글들도 이해하기 시작합니다. 이 학생은 다음과 같은 것을 할 수 있습니다: – 의미를 전달하기 위해 단어들과 구문들 사용 – 사물이나 행동을 설명하기 위해서 제한된 수의 문법 구조를 사용 – 질문과 요청을 하기 시작 – 사건의 단계들로 의사소통하기 시작 – 단어와 문장 발음을 대부분 정확하게 함	실력을 향상시키기 위해서 이 레벨의 학생은: – 익숙한 장소, 물건 그리고 인물들을 묘사하는 단어들을 좀 더 학습합니다. – 일생 생활 주제에 대해 묻고 답하는 연습을 합니다. – 학생이 읽는 이야기 그리고 보는 프로그램에서 발생하는 것들을 문장으로 묘사하는 연습을 합니다.
🎖🎖 5개중 2개의 리본	이 레벨의 학생은 기초 단어들을 인지하기 시작합니다. 이 학생은 다음과 같은 것을 할 수 있습니다: – 집, 학교, 가족, 색, 동물, 행동 등과 같은 익숙한 카테고리 안의 일상적인 단어들 말하기 – 짧고 간단한 문장으로 의사소통 (예: The tiger is big, The zoo has two birds.) – 단어들과 구문들을 정확하지만 가끔 느리게 발음	실력을 향상시키기 위해서 이 레벨의 학생은: – 익숙한 장소, 물건 그리고 인물들을 묘사하는 단어들을 좀 더 학습합니다. – 일상 생활 주제에 대해 묻고 답하는 연습을 합니다. – 학생이 읽는 이야기 그리고 보는 프로그램에서 발생하는 것들을 묘사하는 연습을 합니다.
🎖 5개중 1개의 리본	이 레벨의 학생은 기초 단어들을 이해하기 시작합니다. 이 학생은 다음과 같은 것을 할 수 있습니다: – 집, 학교, 가족, 색, 동물, 행동 등과 같은 익숙한 카테고리 안의 일상적인 단어들 말하기 – 간단한 구문으로 말하기	실력을 향상시키기 위해서 이 레벨의 학생은: – 일상적인 단어들을 학습하고 연습합니다. – 그림에서 보이는 것의 이름을 말합니다. (예: I see a house.) – 학생이 좋아하는 물건, 활동에 대해서 문장으로 말하는 연습을 합니다.
5개중 0개의 리본	이 레벨의 학생은 시험에 응답하지 않았거나 영어로 대답하지 않았습니다.	

Introduction to the TOEFL Junior® Speaking Tests

Test Structure

평가영역	문항 수	시험시간
Speaking	4	18분

TestSection – TOEFL Junior® Speaking Test

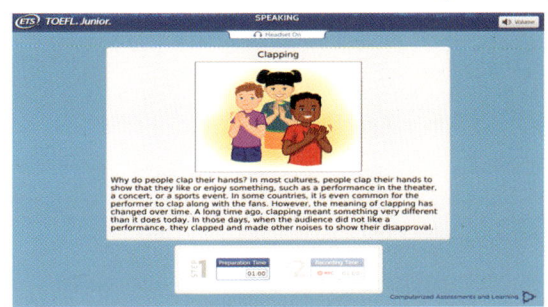

소리내어 읽기
짧은 문단을 1분 동안 연습한 뒤 마이크에 대고 해당 문단을 1분 동안 읽어야 합니다.

그림 묘사
6가지 그림을 보고 그림들이 보여주는 이야기를 말할 것입니다. 1분 동안 이야기를 준비한 후 마이크에 대고 1분 동안 당신의 이야기를 녹음합니다.

듣고 말하기 (학교 관련 주제)
선생님 혹은 학생들이 학교와 관련된 주제에 대해 이야기하는 것을 듣고 당신이 들은 것을 말해야 합니다.
당신은 듣는 동안 메모할 수 있습니다. 당신은 45초 동안 준비하고 이어서 1분 동안 마이크에 대고 당신의 대답을 녹음합니다.

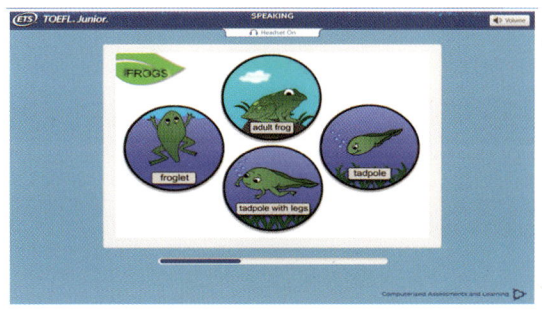

듣고 말하기 (학술적인 주제)
학술적 주제에 대해 선생님이 이야기하는 것을 듣고 당신이 들은 것에 대하여 말해야 합니다.
당신은 듣는 동안 메모할 수 있습니다. 당신은 45초 동안 준비하고 이어서 1분 동안 마이크에 대고 당신의 대답을 녹음합니다.

Test Score Guide – TOEFL Junior® Speaking Test

점수 범위	시험 평가 설명	CEFR 레벨
14–16	거의 항상 적절하고, 다양하고 효과적인 어휘와 문법을 사용하며 항상 청취자는 이해한다.	B2
11–13	보통 적절하고 효과적인 어휘와 문법을 사용하며 보통 청취자는 이해한다.	B1
8–10	가끔 청취자가 이해할 수 있는 말을 할 수 있다.	A2
8 아래	기초 어휘와 단순 문법 구조를 구사할 수 있다.	A2 아래

- 점수는 0점에서 16점 사이입니다.
- 점수 범위별로 영어 실력 설명과 다음 단계를 위한 추천 영어 학습법이 각 단계별로 제공되고 있습니다.
- 설명서에 나온 점수 범위에 따른 영어 실력 설명과 다음 단계를 위한 추천 영어 공부 방법은 각 레벨에 맞추어 져 있으며, 모든 학생들을 위한 방법이 아닙니다.
- 각 레벨의 학생들은 자신 보다 낮은 레벨의 학생들이 갖춘 영어 실력을 갖추고 있다는 뜻도 됩니다.
- 학생의 실력을 평가할 수 있는 CEFR 레벨을 같이 제공합니다.

About Preparation Book for the TOEFL Primary® Speaking

ETS TOEFL Primary® Speaking Test 대비서로써 실제 시험과 같이 1가지 주제를 기준으로 여러 유형의 문제를 학습할 수 있도록 구성되어 있습니다.

단어학습부터 듣기, 쓰기 연습을 거쳐 최적의 답변을 말할 수 있도록 설계되어 있으며, 마지막 Actual Test 2회분을 수록하여 실전 감각을 익힐 수 있도록 하였습니다.

또한 이 책에서 내가 직접 주인공이 되어 다양한 문제에 대한 답변을 함으로써, 자연스럽게 영어 말하기에 대한 흥미와 자신감을 높일 수 있습니다.

※ 문제 별 Sample Answer 제공 (mp3 포함)

❯ How to Use This Book

Vocabulary Practice / 단어학습

- Brainstorm : 주제에 맞는 단어 생각하기
- 빈칸 채우기 : 문장에 알맞은 단어 쓰기
- Your Turn : 내 생각 쓰고, 말하기

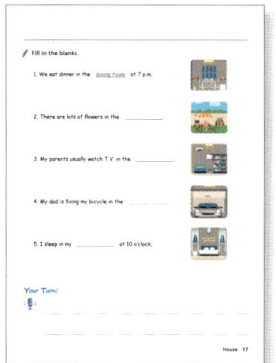

Expressing Opinions / 표현하기

- 사진을 보고, 좋아하는 것 말하기
- 제시된 그림을 보고, 좋아하는 이유 말하기

1 - 문장에 알맞은 답 쓰고 말하기
2 - Your Turn (내 생각 쓰고, 말하기)

Making Requests / 요청하기

- 제시된 것을 보고, 상황에 맞게 요청하기

1 - 문장에 알맞은 답 쓰고 말하기
2 - Your Turn (내 생각 쓰고, 말하기)

Describing a Picture / 설명하기

- 사진을 보고, 이상한 부분 설명하기

1 - 알맞은 문장 연결하기
2 - 연결한 문장 이어서 쓰고, 말하기
3 - Your Turn (내 생각 쓰고, 말하기)

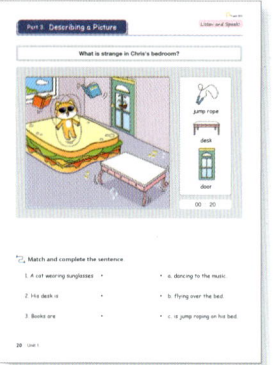 

Asking Questions / 질문하기

- 사진을 보고, 3가지 질문하기

1 - 순서에 맞춰 문장 완성하고, 말하기
2 - Your Turn (내 생각 쓰고, 말하기)

Giving Directions / 지시하기

- 4컷의 그림을 보고, 지시사항 말하기

1 - 문장 순서 맞추기
2 - Your Turn (순서에 맞춰 문장 쓰고, 말하기)

12

Retelling a Story / 서술하기

- 6컷의 그림을 보고, 상황 서술하기
  (실제 시험에서는 동영상으로 출제)

 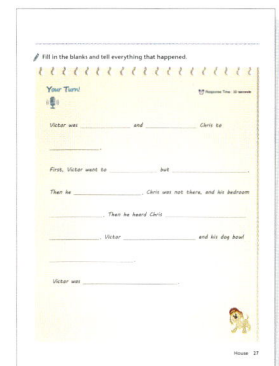

Presentation / 발표하기

- 주제에 맞는 다양한 활동 후 발표하기

✽ 실제 시험에 출제되지 않으나, 해당 활동을 통해 나만의 포트폴리오를 갖게 됩니다.

Word Test / 단어시험

- 각 Unit 별로 학습한 단어 복습하기

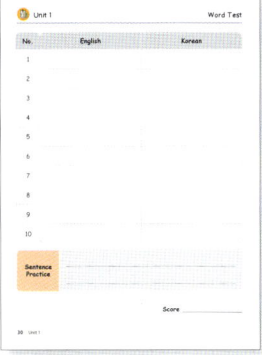

Actual Test / 2회분

- 실제 시험과 비슷한 환경에서 실전 연습하기

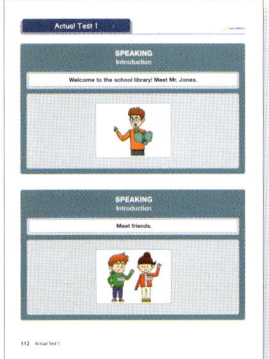 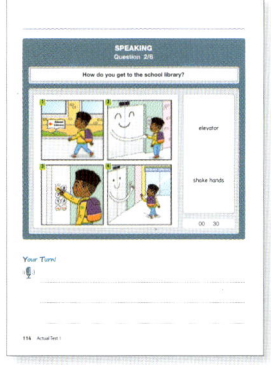

Characters

Your picture

Your Name

Narrator

Jack

Friends

Chris   Julie   Kevin

School Pet

Max

Teachers

Science Teacher
Ms. Smith

Librarian
Mr. Jones

Art Teacher
Ms. Perry

Unit 1 House

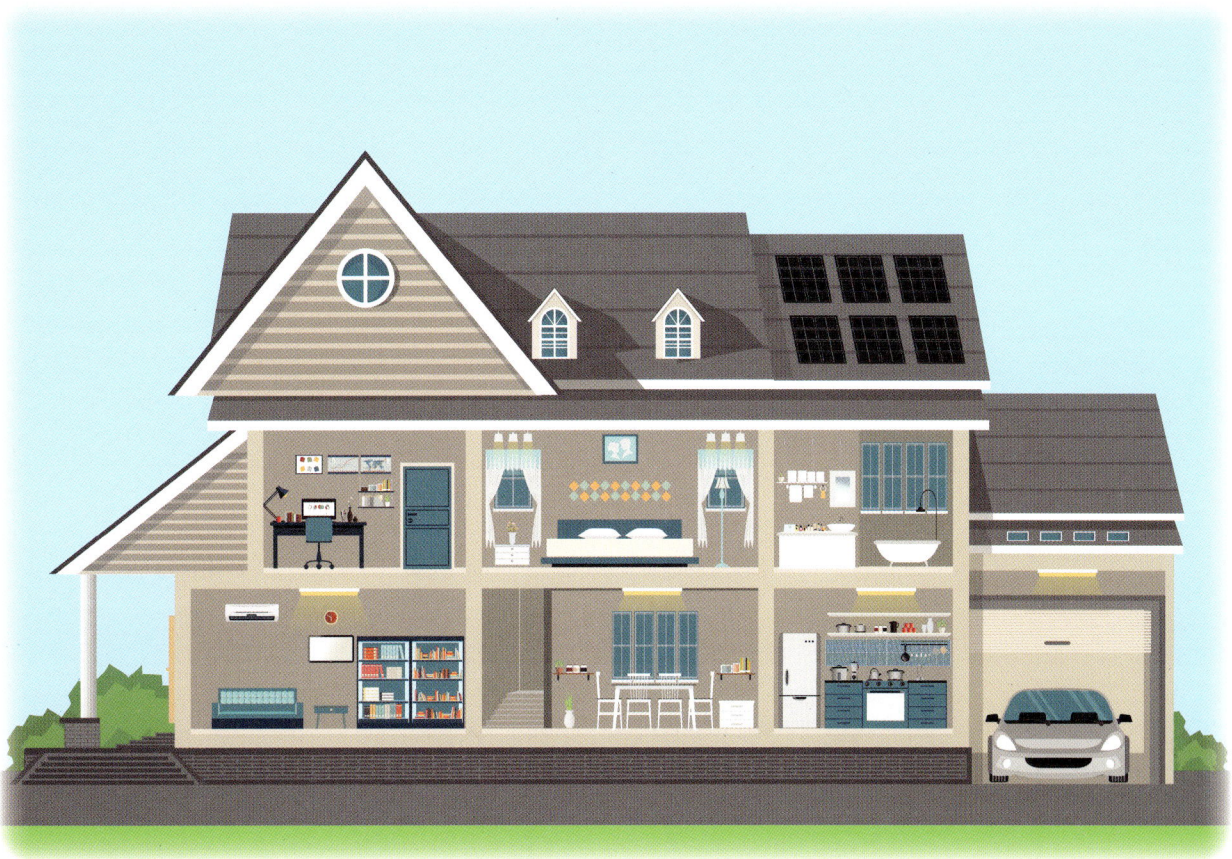

Hi! I am Jack.
I am going to visit Chris with you.

Welcome to my house.
We have lots of things to do today.
Let's have fun!

Vocabulary Practice

Track 002
Listen and Repeat!

✏️ Brainstorm and fill in the bubbles.

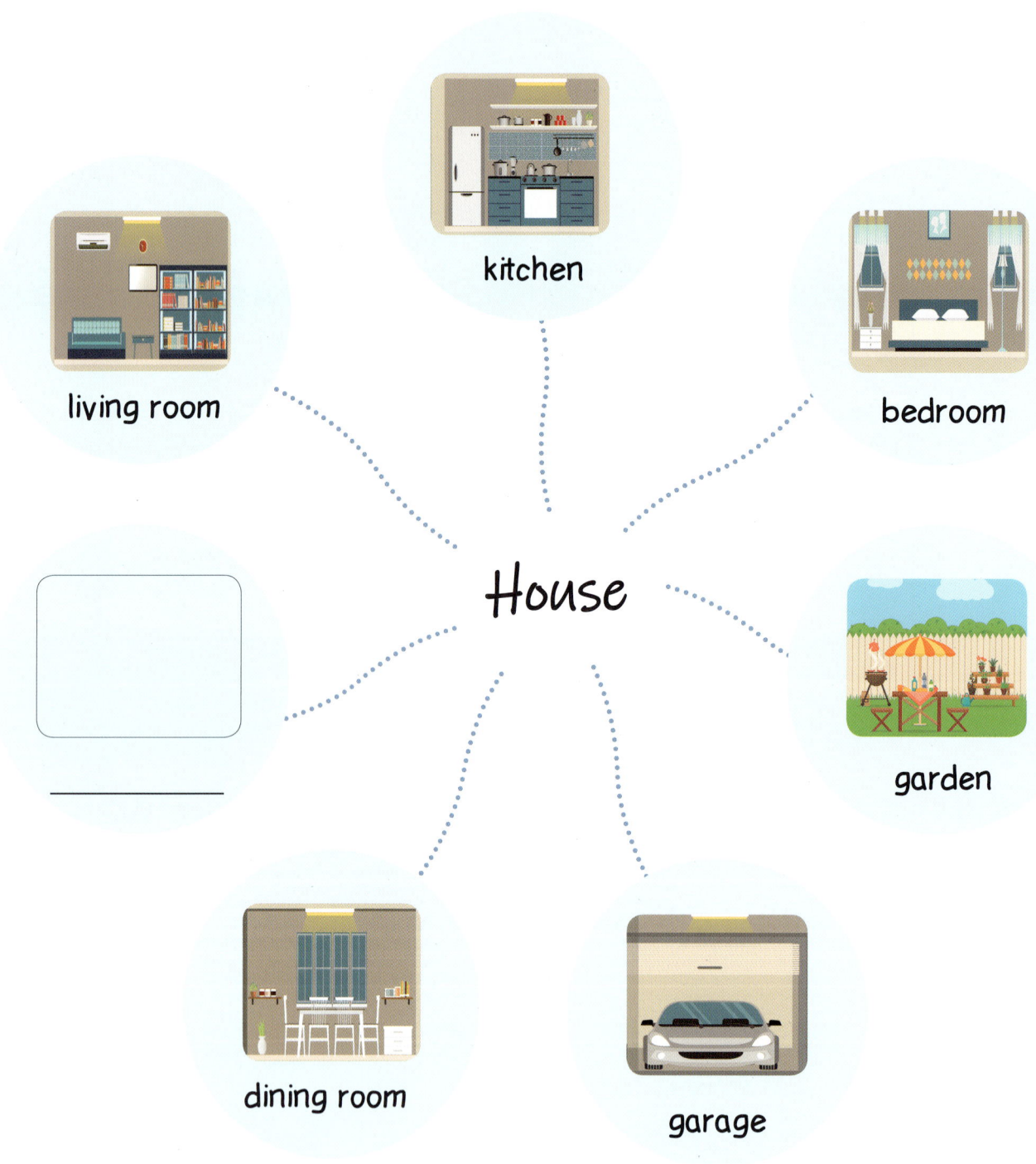

Unit 1

✏️ **Fill in the blanks.**

1. We eat dinner in the   dining room   at 7 p.m.

2. There are lots of flowers in the _____.

3. My parents usually watch T.V. in the _____.

4. My dad is fixing my bicycle in the _____.

5. I sleep in my _____ at 10 o'clock.

Your Turn!

Track 003

Part 1. Expressing Opinions

Listen and Speak!

What do you like to do?

00 : 10

✏️ **Fill in the blanks using the Key Chunk.**

- I like to   <u>play video games</u>   with my friend because it is more exciting than playing them alone.

- I like to   w_____   with my friend. It is more fun to watch T.V. together.

Your Turn!

⏰ Response Time : 10 seconds

📌 **Key Chunk**

| do one's homework | have a snack | play a video game | watch T.V. |

18   Unit 1

Part 2. Making Requests

Listen and Speak!

Track 004

Ask to get some water.

00 : 15

✏️ **Fill in the blanks using the Key Chunk.**

- Chris, I am so thirsty. <u>Can I</u> have some water?

- Chris, c_____ get me some water? I am so thirsty.

Your Turn!

Response Time : 15 seconds

Key Chunk

| can you please ~ ? | get me some water | have some water |

House 19

Part 3. Describing a Picture

Track 005
Listen and Speak!

What is strange in Chris's bedroom?

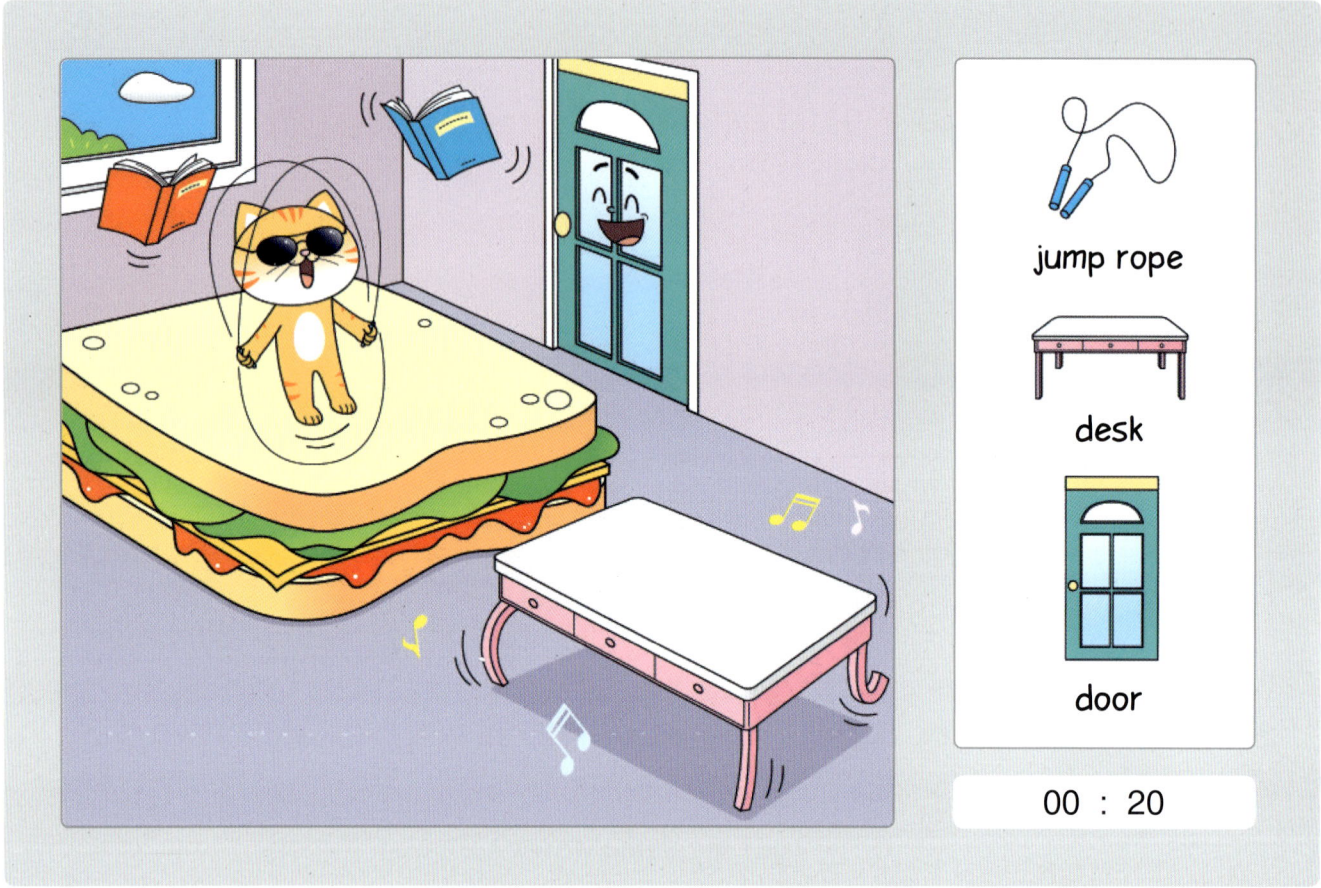

00 : 20

Match and complete the sentence.

1. A cat wearing sunglasses is •   • a. dancing to the music.

2. His desk is •   • b. flying over the bed.

3. Books are •   • c. jumping rope on his bed.

20   Unit 1

✏️ **Write and tell everything that is strange in Chris's bedroom using Match and complete the sentence.**

Chris's bedroom is very strange.

First,

Your Turn!

⏰ Response Time : 20 seconds

Part 4. Asking Questions

🎧 Track 006

Listen and Speak!

Questions about the Chris's family picture

00 : 30

 **Key Chunk**

| get married | how many | how old | how tall | take a picture |

22   Unit 1

✏️ **Make sentences using the Key Chunk.**

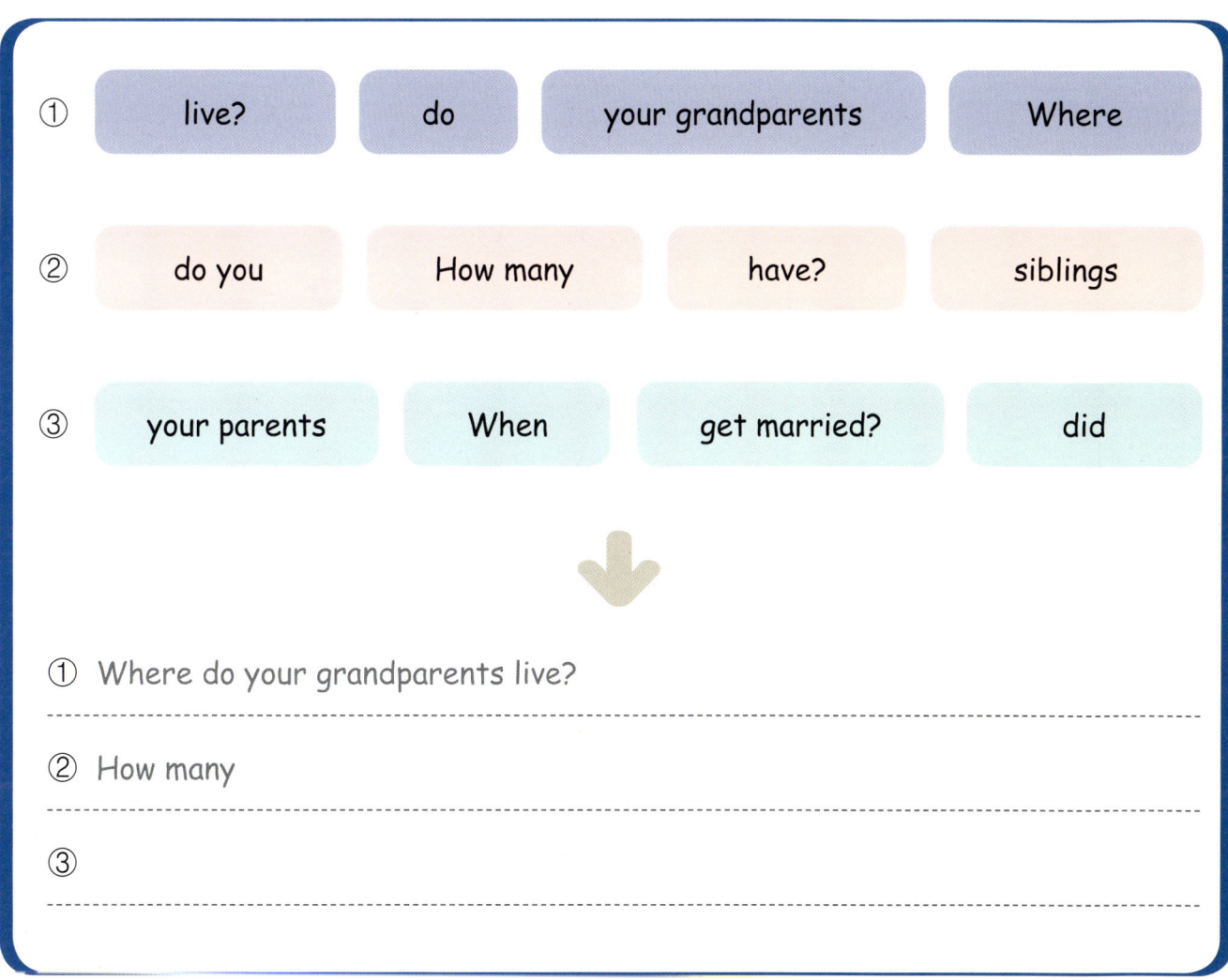

① Where do your grandparents live?

② How many

③

Your Turn!

Response Time : 30 seconds

①

②

③

Part 5. Giving Directions

Track 007
Listen and Speak!

How do you feed the dog?

cupboard

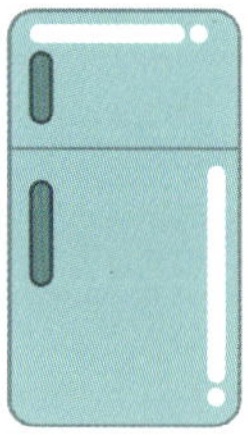

fridge

dog bowl

00 : 30

 Key Chunk

| call out | in a loud voice | pour water | put into | take out |

24   Unit 1

Number the sentences in the correct order.

( ) Last, call out your dog in a loud voice. "Victor! Your lunch is ready!"

( ) And put some dog food into one of the dog bowls.

( ) Then, pour some water into the other bowl.

(1) First, you need to take out the dog food from the cupboard.

Your Turn!

Response Time : 30 seconds

Part 6. Retelling a Story

Track 008

Listen and Speak!

What happened? What did Victor do?

dining room

bedroom

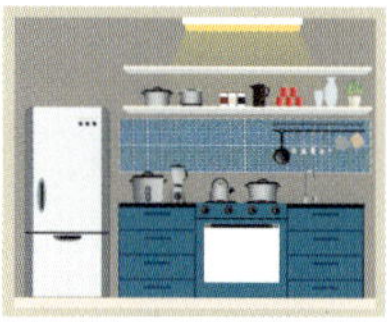

kitchen

00 : 30

Key Chunk

ask for   call someone's name   full of   look for   run to

26   Unit 1

✏️ **Fill in the blanks and tell everything that happened.**

Your Turn!

🎤

⏰ Response Time : 30 seconds

Victor was _____ and _____ Chris to _____.

First, Victor went to _____ but _____.

Then he _____. Chris was not there, and his bedroom _____. Then he heard Chris _____. Victor _____ and his dog bowl _____.

Victor was _____.

Presentation

 Draw your dream house.

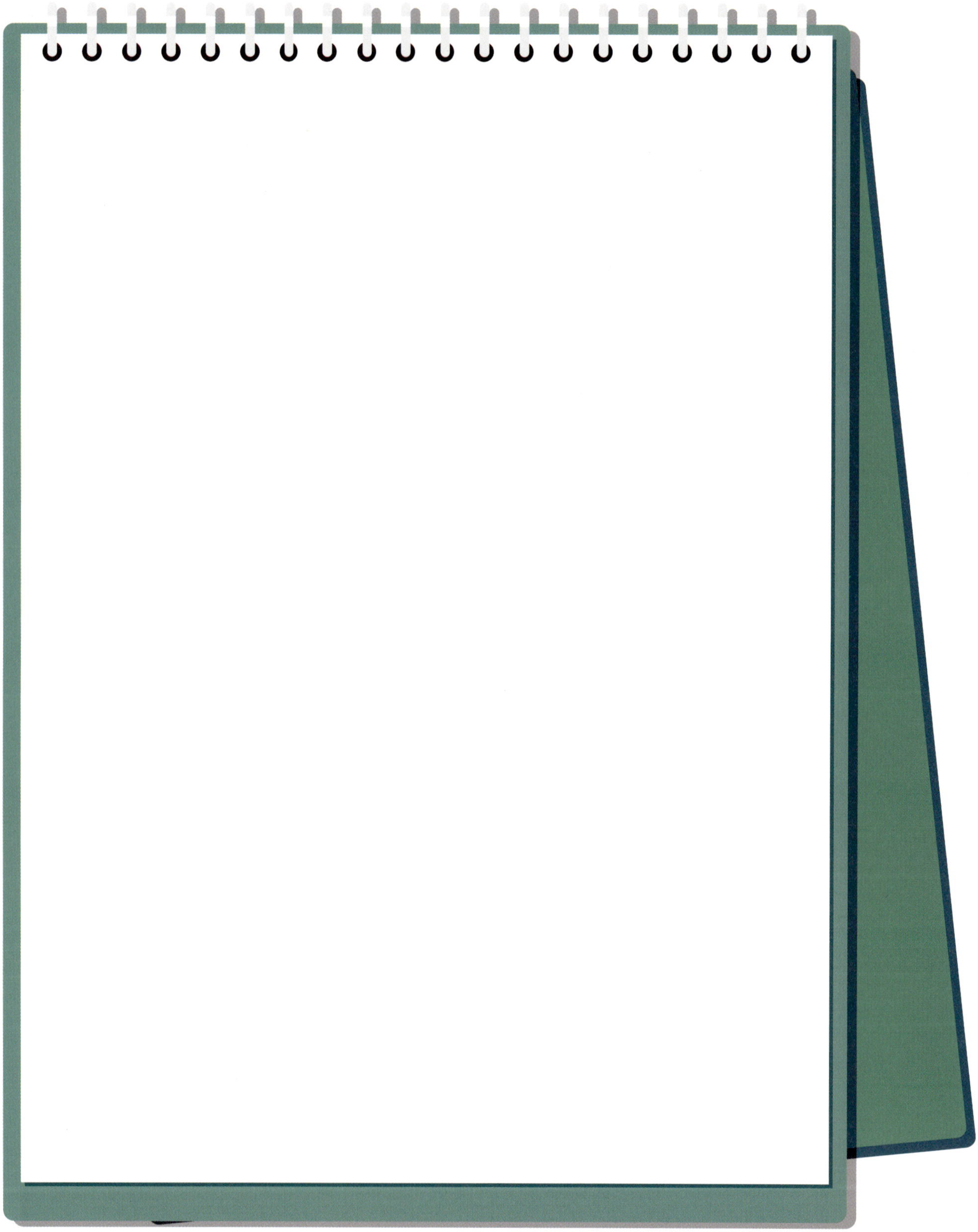

✏️ **Write and present your dream house.**

My dream house has / is ......

 **Unit 1**   **Word Test**

No.	English	Korean
1		
2		
3		
4		
5		
6		
7		
8		
9		
10		

Sentence Practice

Score _____

Unit 2 Vacation

Track 009

It's summer vacation!
Do you like camping? Let's go camping!

I love camping!
Let's go camping!

Vocabulary Practice

Track 010
Listen and Repeat!

✏️ Brainstorm and fill in the bubbles.

✏️ **Fill in the blanks.**

1. I often <u>go camping</u> and hiking with my family.

2. Can I help you _____ your things?

3. Spending time in _____ makes me feel happier.

4. I listen to music to _____ stress.

5. They built a sandcastle at the _____.

Your Turn!

🎤

🎧 Track 011

Part 1. Expressing Opinions

Listen and Speak!

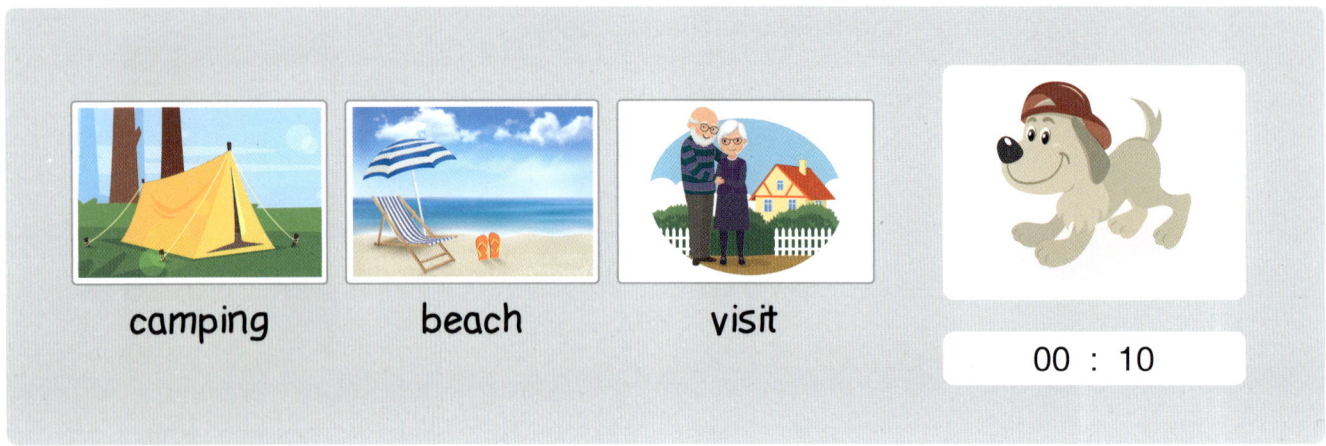

What do you like to do during vacation?

camping   beach   visit

00 : 10

✏️ **Fill in the blanks using the Key Chunk.**

- I like to <u>go camping</u> with my family during vacation because I like spending time in _____.

- I like to go to the <u>b_____</u> during vacation. I can <u>b_____</u> at the beach.

Your Turn!

⏰ Response Time : 10 seconds

🎤

🛩️ Key Chunk

| build a sandcastle | go camping | go abroad | spend time | visit relatives |

34   Unit 2

Part 2. Making Requests

Listen and Speak!

Ask your mom if you can go camping with Julie's family.

00 : 15

✏️ Fill in the blanks using the Key Chunk.

- Mom, can I go camping with Julie's family _____?

- Mom, Jack is _____ with Julie's family this weekend. _____ with them?

Your Turn!

Response Time : 15 seconds

 Key Chunk

| go camping | can I go ~ ? | this weekend |

Part 3. Describing a Picture

Listen and Speak! — Track 013

What is strange in the boat?

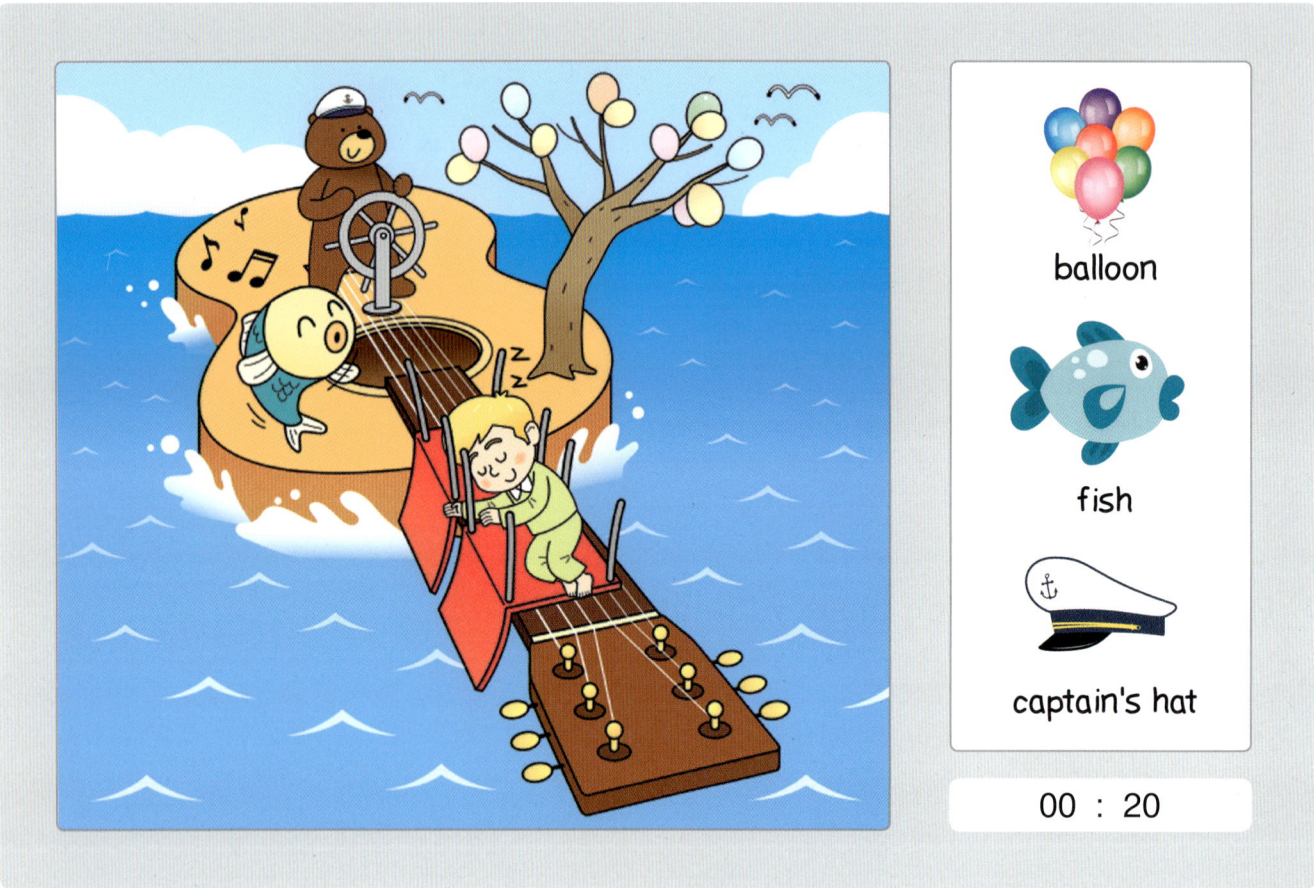

Match and complete the sentence.

1. There is • • a. a big balloon tree in the middle of the boat.

2. The shape of the boat is • • b. wearing a captain's hat.

3. A bear is • • c. a guitar.

Write and tell everything that is strange in the boat using Match and complete the sentence.

The boat is very strange.

First,

Your Turn!

Response Time : 20 seconds

Part 4. Asking Questions

🎧 Track 014

Listen and Speak!

Questions about the big tree

00 : 30

Key Chunk

| how many | how tall | kinds of | how old |

✏️ **Make sentences using the Key Chunk.**

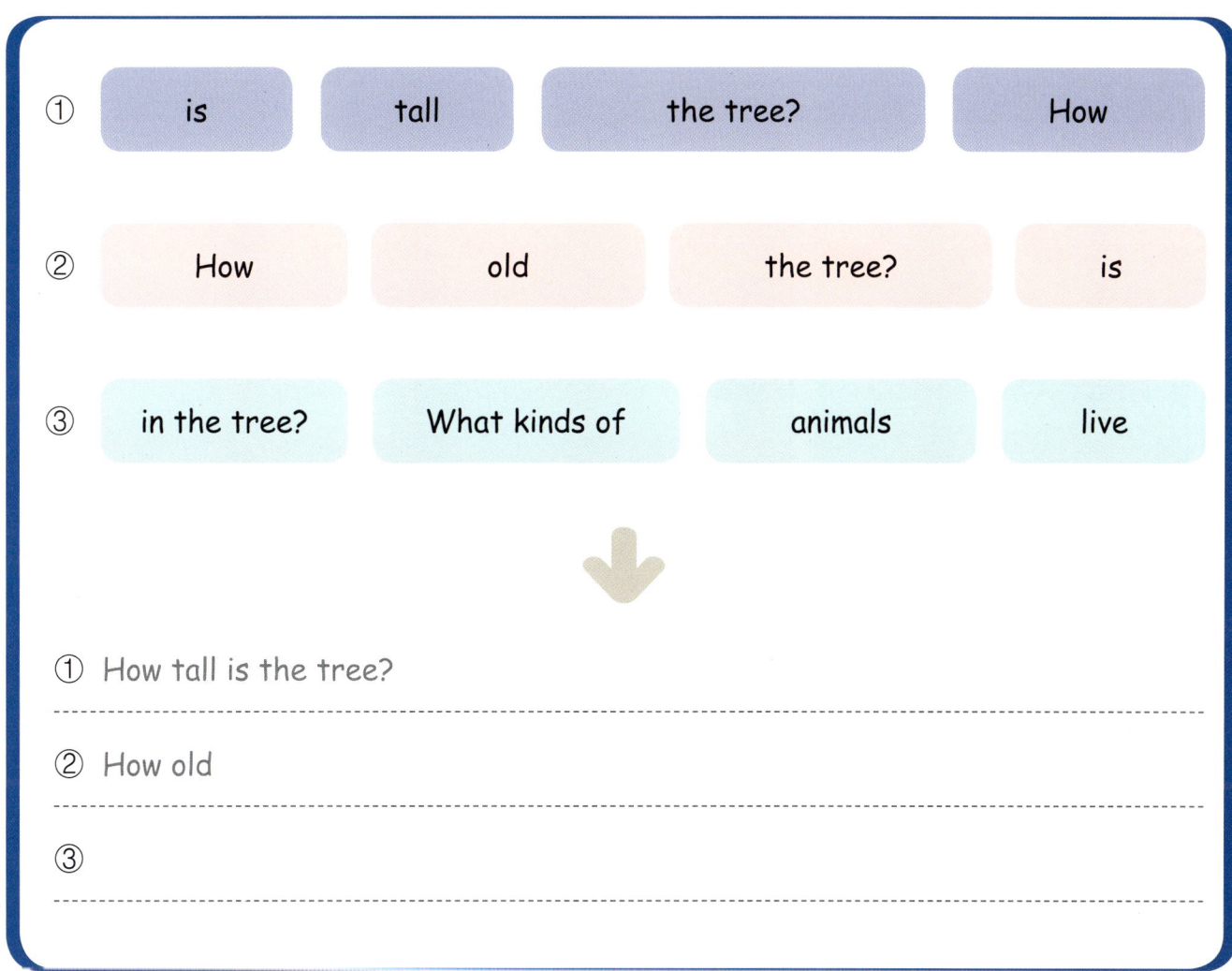

① How tall is the tree?

② How old

③

Your Turn! Response Time : 30 seconds

①

②

③

🎧 Track 015

Part 5. Giving Directions

Listen and Speak!

How do you fish in the lake?

fishing rod

chair

lake

00 : 30

 Key Chunk

cast a fishing rod　　　get caught　　　pull out　　　prepare for　　　set up

40　Unit 2

Number the sentences in the correct order.

- **1** First, you need to set up a chair and a fishing rod by the lakeside.

- Sit down on the chair and wait.

- Finally, when fish gets caught, strongly pull out the fishing rod.

- Then, cast the fishing rod into the lake as far as you can.

Your Turn!

Response Time : 30 seconds

Part 6. Retelling a Story

Track 016
Listen and Speak!

What happened? What did the animals do?

dish

grilled corn

snatch

00 : 30

▸ **Key Chunk**

be ready   delicious dishes   nothing is left   run away   take something

42   Unit 2

✏️ **Fill in the blanks and tell everything that happened.**

Your Turn!

🎤

⏰ Response Time : 30 seconds

Dinner <u>was ready</u>. There were many _____ on the table. But a rabbit appeared and _____. Then a brown bear came. He _____ and _____ to the forest. Next, a fox came and _____. Last, an eagle _____ and _____. The animals _____. _____ and the table is empty now.

Presentation

Complete the Thinking Map.

- My summer vacation
  - Take _____
  - Arrive at _____
  - _____

Key Chunk

 take a train

 arrive at the campsite

 go fishing

 have dinner

✏️ **Write and present your vacation.**

During last summer vacation, I went

It was amazing. I had really good time.

Unit 2 — Word Test

No.	English	Korean
1		
2		
3		
4		
5		
6		
7		
8		
9		
10		

Sentence Practice

Score _____

Unit 3 Lunch Break!

Track 017

It's 12 o'clock. Lunch break! What do you do during the lunch break?

I am hungry. Let's go to the cafeteria!

Track 018

Vocabulary Practice

Listen and Repeat!

✏️ Brainstorm and fill in the bubbles.

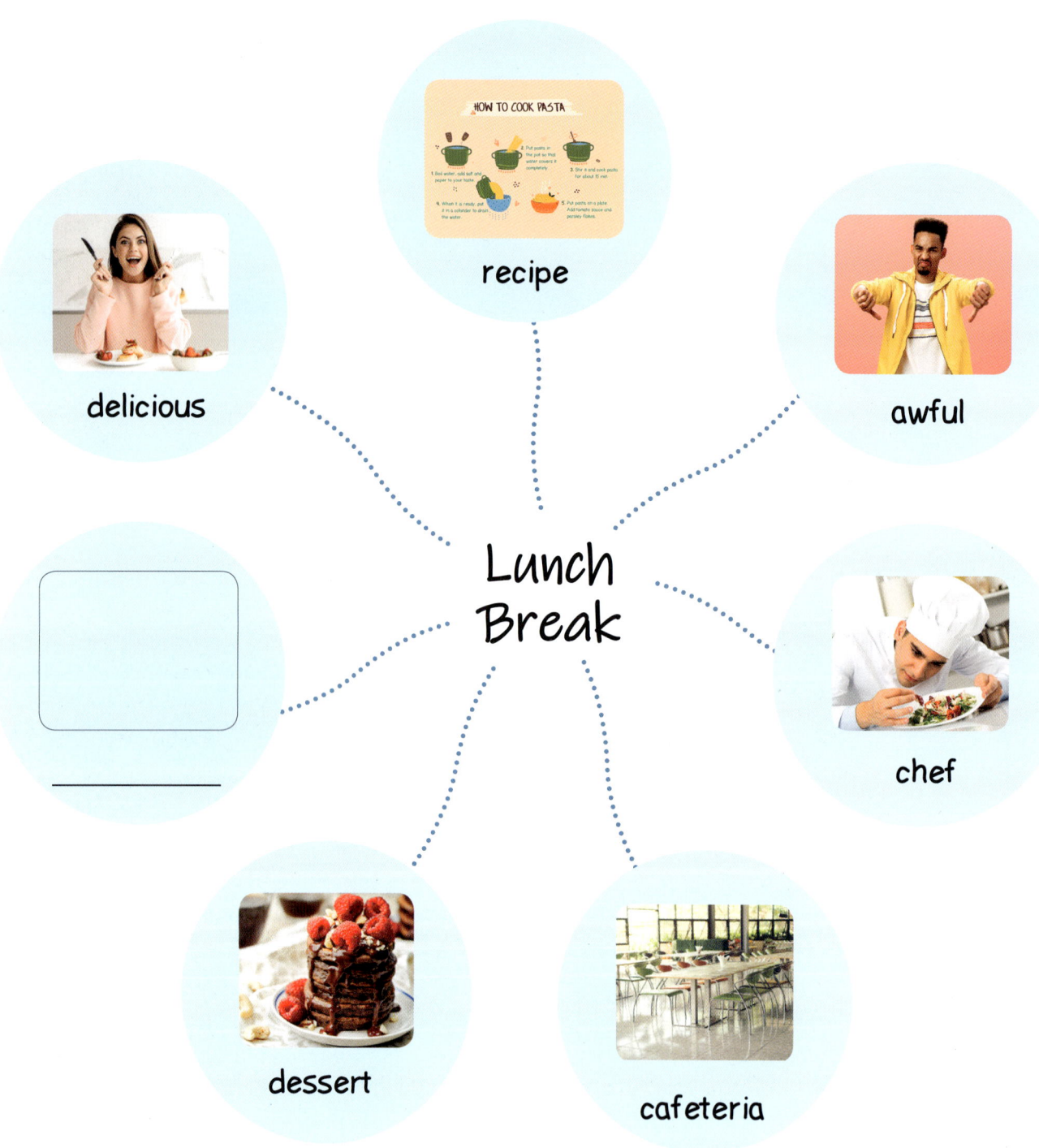

48　Unit 3

Fill in the blanks.

1. Some students are eating lunch in the <u>cafeteria</u>.

2. Chocolate cake is my favorite _____.

3. He served us a _____ dinner.

4. I am sure you'll be a great _____.

5. This chicken soup tastes _____. I can't eat this soup.

Your Turn!

Part 1. Expressing Opinions

🎧 Track 019
Listen and Speak!

Which food do you like?

curry   hamburger   sushi

00 : 10

✏️ **Fill in the blanks using the Key Chunk.**

- I like   curry   because it is   healthy food .
- I _____ hamburgers _____ because they _____.

Your Turn!

⏰ Response Time : 10 seconds

🎤

✈️ **Key Chunk**

| healthy food | junk food | like best | taste bad | taste good |

50   Unit 3

Part 2. Making Requests

🎧 Track 020

Listen and Speak!

Ask to get more chocolate cookies.

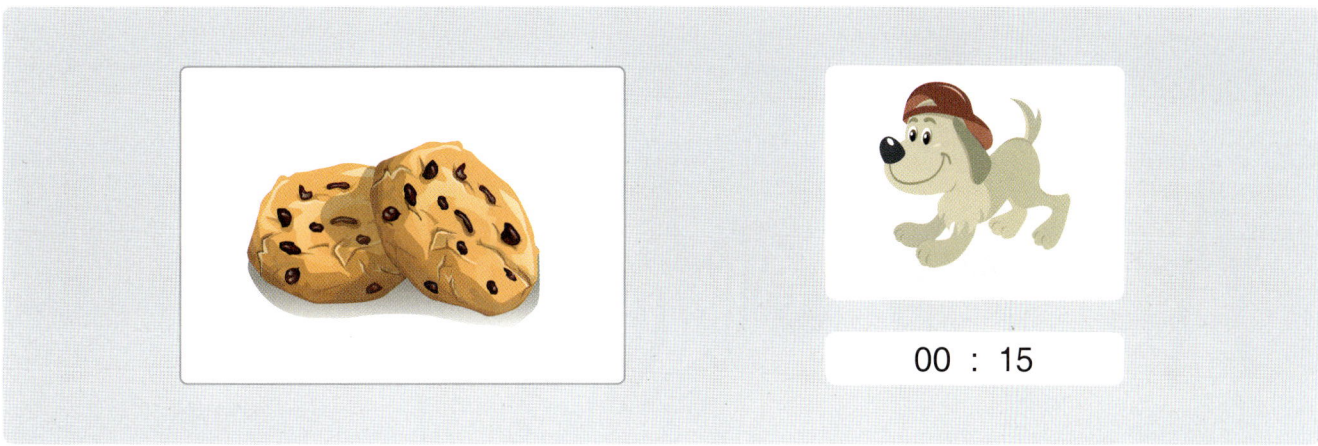

00 : 15

✏️ **Fill in the blanks using Key Chunk.**

- C_____ give me more dessert? I love these chocolate cookies.
- Can I g_____ chocolate cookies? They're my f_____ .

Your Turn!

⏰ Response Time : 15 seconds

🔖 Key Chunk

| could you~? | can you please ~ ? | get more | favorite dessert |

Lunch Break!

Part 3. Describing a Picture

🎧 Track 021

Listen and Speak!

What is strange in the playground?

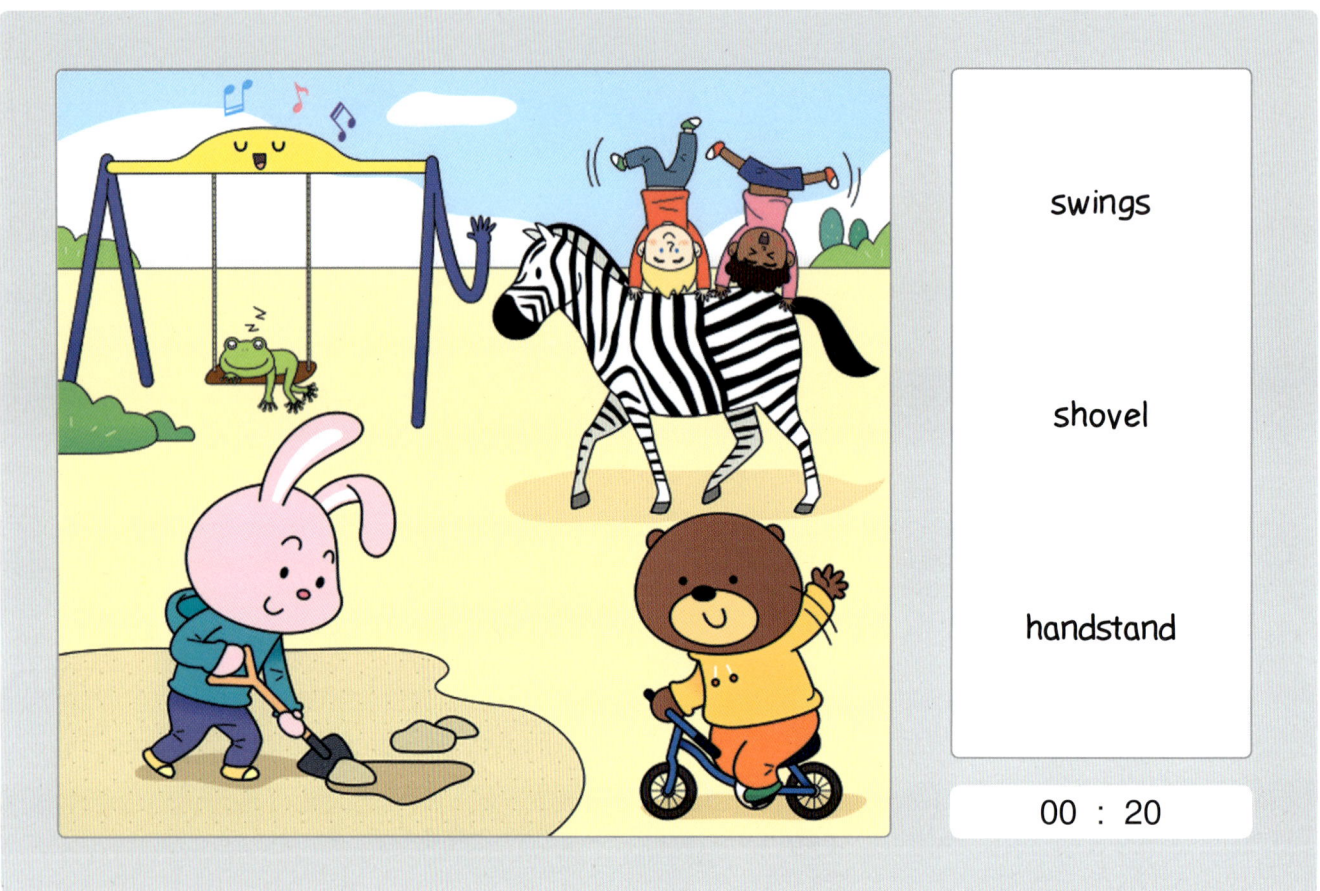

00 : 20

🔗 **Match and complete the sentence.**

1. A frog is sleeping •   • a. with a shovel.

2. A rabbit is digging a hole •   • b. on the swings.

3. Kids are doing a handstand •   • c. on a zebra.

52   Unit 3

✏️ **Write and tell everything that is strange in the playground using Match and complete the sentence.**

The playground is very strange.

First,

Your Turn!

⏰ Response Time : 20 seconds

Lunch Break! 53

🎧 Track 022

Part 4. Asking Questions

Listen and Speak!

Questions about basketball

00 : 30

 **Key Chunk**

| how many players | playing basketball | get points | how do you prepare |

54   Unit 3

✏️ **Make sentences using the Key Chunk.**

① | on a basketball team? | are | players | How many |

② | What do you | need for | basketball? | playing |

③ | points | in basketball ? | How do you | get |

⬇

① How many players are on a basketball team?
----
②   playing basketball?
----
③

Your Turn!

🎙️ ①
----
②
----
③

Response Time : 30 seconds

Lunch Break! 55

Part 5. Giving Directions

Track 023

Listen and Speak!

How do you play basketball?

referee

bounce

hoop

00 : 30

Key Chunk

high up   continuously   stretch   by shooting

Unit 3

Number the sentences in the correct order.

- ( ) A basketball game starts at the center of the court when the ball is thrown high up by the referee.

- ( ) Use one hand to bounce the basketball continuously to move the ball.

- (1) Before starting a basketball game, stretch your body first.

- ( ) Last, score points by shooting the ball through the hoop.

Your Turn!

Response Time : 30 seconds

Lunch Break! 57

Part 6. Retelling a Story

🎧 Track 024

Listen and Speak!

What happened? What did Max do?

white board

mess

00 : 30

Key Chunk

sneak out of   sneak into   scribbled on   mess   school pet

58   Unit 3

✏️ **Fill in the blanks and tell everything that happened.**

Your Turn!

🎙️

⏰ Response Time : 30 seconds

The classroom was _____. Then Max, the

school pet, _____. He ate _____ and

drank _____. And then he

_____. He scribbled _____

and threw things. Soon the _____ and the

school bell rang. Max _____ the classroom.

Lunch Break! 59

Presentation

 Pasta is my favorite dish. I sometimes help my mom to cook pasta. Here is my pasta recipe.

Ingredients : pasta, tomato sauce, parsley flakes
Equipment : pot, colander, plate

✏️ **Write and present the recipe for your favorite dish.**

My favorite dish is _____.

Ingredients

Equipment

Instructions

First,

Then,

Next,

Then,

Finally,

Enjoy your meal!

Lunch Break!

Unit 3 — Word Test

No.	English	Korean
1		
2		
3		
4		
5		
6		
7		
8		
9		
10		

Sentence Practice

Score _____

Unit 4 Field Trip

Where do you want to go for a field trip?

I want to go to an art museum. Do you want to come with us?

Vocabulary Practice

Listen and Repeat!
Track 026

✏️ Brainstorm and fill in the bubbles.

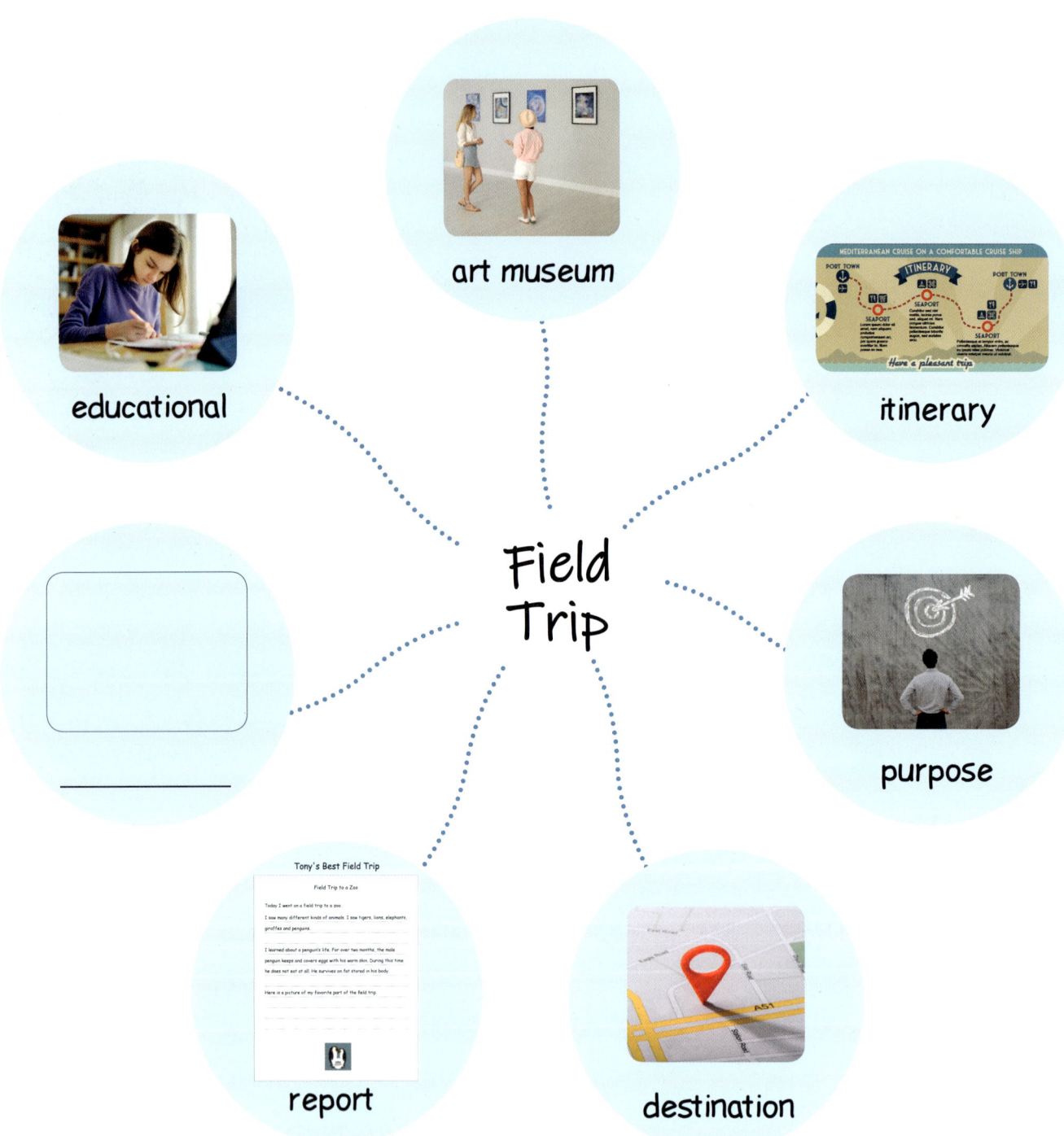

✏️ **Fill in the blanks.**

1. Our   destination   was the palace.

2. Going on a field trip can be very _____.

3. The _____ is showing famous paintings.

4. What is the _____ of this field trip?

5. Do you have your trip _____ with you?

Your Turn!

Field Trip 65

Part 1. Expressing Opinions

🎧 Track 027
Listen and Speak!

What do you like about field trips?

00 : 10

✏️ **Fill in the blanks using the Key Chunk.**

- I like visiting <u>interesting places</u> on a field trip.

- I like _____ with my classmates during a field trip.

Your Turn!

⏰ Response Time : 10 seconds

🔖 **Key Chunk**

| experience new things | hang out | have fun | interesting places |

66   Unit 4

Part 2. Making Requests

🎧 Track 028

Listen and Speak!

Ask to go to an art museum.

00 : 15

✏️ **Fill in the blanks using the Key Chunk.**

- Ms. Perry, can we go to an art museum   <u>for a field trip</u>? We can see many <u>famous paintings</u>   in the museum.

- Ms. Perry,   <u>c_____</u>   take us to an observatory for a field trip? We want to _____ the stars.

Your Turn!

⏰ Response Time : 15 seconds

🔖 Key Chunk

| could you~? | famous painting | for a field trip | learn about |

Field Trip   67

Part 3. Describing a Picture

Track 029
Listen and Speak!

What is strange in the European Art room?

Match and complete the sentence.

1. Frogs are • • a. looking at the paintings.

2. The Thinker is • • b. sitting on the nest.

3. The ceiling lights are • • c. oranges.

✏️ **Write and tell everything that is strange in the European Art room using Match and complete the sentence.**

European Art room is very strange.

First,

Your Turn!

🕐 Response Time : 20 seconds

Field Trip 69

Track 030

Listen and Speak!

Part 4. Asking Questions

Questions about the vase

vase

00 : 30

 Key Chunk

| be used for | come from | how old | made of |

70   Unit 4

✏️ **Make sentences using the Key Chunk.**

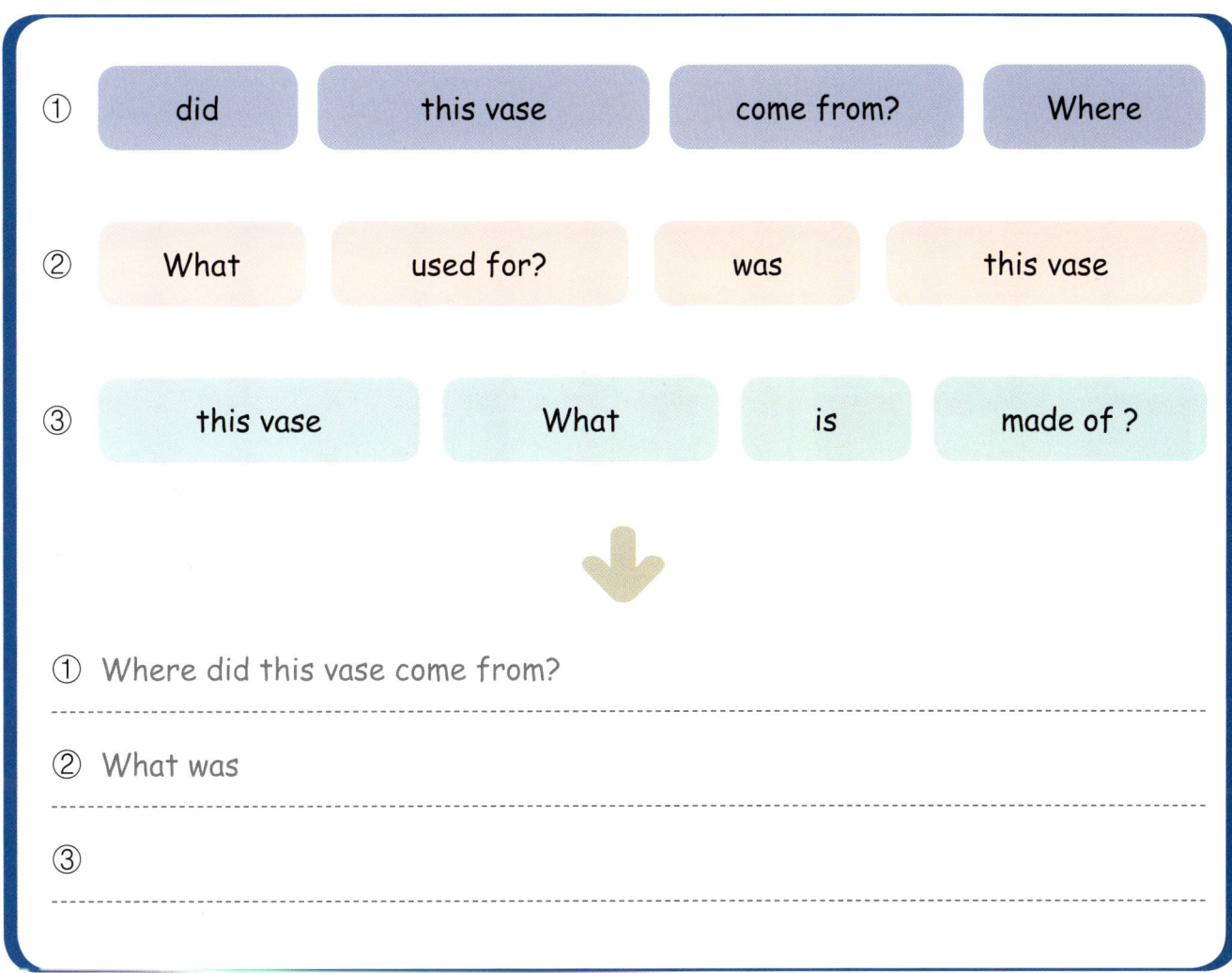

① did | this vase | come from? | Where

② What | used for? | was | this vase

③ this vase | What | is | made of ?

⬇

① Where did this vase come from?
---
② What was
---
③

Your Turn!

🕐 Response Time : 30 seconds

🎙 ①
---
②
---
③

Field Trip 71

Part 5. Giving Directions

🎧 Track 031

Listen and Speak!

How do you complete the worksheet?

worksheet

in front of

00 : 30

**Key Chunk**

complete the worksheet　　　hand out　　　line up　　　listen to　　　look around

72　Unit 4

Number the sentences in the correct order.

- ( ) Last, we can look around in the museum and complete the worksheet.
- (1) First, listen to Ms. Perry carefully while she explains how to complete the worksheet.
- ( ) Then, we need to prepare a pencil and line up in front of her.
- ( ) When we receive the worksheet, we should write down our name on it.

Your Turn!

Response Time : 30 seconds

Field Trip

Part 6. Retelling a Story

🎧 Track 032

Listen and Speak!

What happened? What did Max do?

hide

lollipop

branch

00 : 30

Key Chunk

treasure map   climb up a tree   lots of   in someone's hands   look for

74   Unit 4

✏️ **Fill in the blanks and tell everything that happened.**

Your Turn!

🕗 Response Time : 30 seconds

Max had lots of treats _____. He wanted to

_____ and was _____ some places.

_____ in the garden and _____.

Then, he hid some chocolates _____ and covered them

with _____.

Next, he drew a _____ and _____.

Field Trip 75

Presentation

✏️ **Read Tony's best field trip.**

Tony's Best Field Trip

Field Trip to a Zoo

Today I went on a field trip to a zoo.

I saw many different kinds of animals. I saw tigers, lions, elephants, giraffes and penguins.

I learned about a penguin's life. For over two months, the male penguin keeps and covers eggs with his warm skin. During this time he does not eat at all. He survives on fat stored in his body.

Here is a picture of my favorite part of the field trip.

✏️ **Write and present your best field trip.**

Name _____ Date _____

My Best Field Trip

I went on _____

I saw

_____

_____

I learned about

_____

_____

_____

Here is a picture of my favorite part of the field trip.

 Unit 4 Word Test

No.	English	Korean
1		
2		
3		
4		
5		
6		
7		
8		
9		
10		

Sentence Practice

Score _____

Unit 5 Shopping Mall

 Track 033

Do you like shopping?
What do you buy at the mall?

I like shopping!
Let's go to the mall.

Shopping Mall 79

Vocabulary Practice

Track 034
Listen and Repeat!

✏️ Brainstorm and fill in the bubbles.

- present 
- downtown
- checkout
- store
- hang out
- window shopping
- _____

Shopping Mall

Fill in the blanks.

1. I bought my brother's birthday   <u>present</u>   yesterday.

2. My mom enjoys _____.

3. Jennifer will _____ with her friends this weekend.

4. You can buy the guitar at the music _____.

5. The new mall is in the _____.

Your Turn!

Shopping Mall 81

Part 1. Expressing Opinions

🎧 Track 035

Listen and Speak!

What do you like about the mall?

00 : 10

✏️ **Fill in the blanks using the Key Chunk.**

- I like window shopping in the shopping mall. I like to see many things.

- I like   h_____   with my friends at the shopping mall because there are many places we can   s_____   together.

Your Turn!

⏰ Response Time : 10 seconds

📎 **Key Chunk**

| different kinds of | many kinds of | hang out | spend time |

82   Unit 5

Part 2. Making Requests

Track 036

Listen and Speak!

Ask to go to the shopping mall.

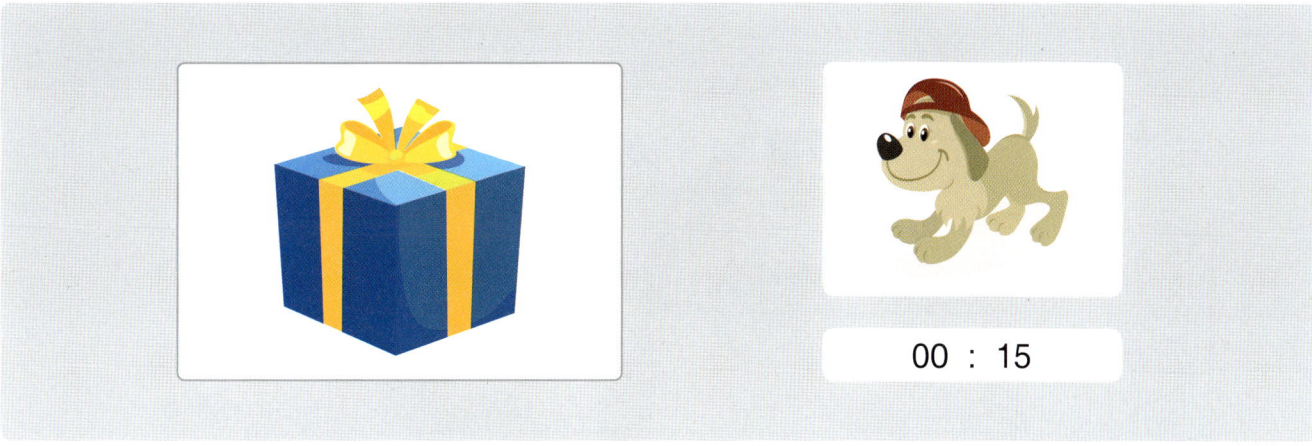

00 : 15

✏️ **Fill in the blanks using the Key Chunk.**

- Mom, <u>can I</u> go to the mall with Julie this Saturday? We need to buy Chris's <u>birthday present</u>.

- Mom, Chris's birthday is _____ and I need to buy a _____. Can I go to the mall with Julie this Saturday?

Your Turn!

⏰ Response Time : 15 seconds

🎤

🔹 **Key Chunk**

| can I ~? | birthday present | present for someone | coming up |

Shopping Mall 83

Part 3. Describing a Picture

Listen and Speak!

Track 037

What is strange in the shoe store?

mirror

giraffe

handstand

00 : 20

Match and complete the sentence.

1. A giraffe is • • a. wearing shoes on their hands.

2. Handstanding kids are • • b. trying on high heels.

3. Shoes are • • c. flying around.

84   Unit 5

✏️ Write and tell everything that is strange in the shoe store using Match and complete the sentence.

The shoe store is very strange.

First,

Your Turn!

Response Time : 20 seconds

Part 4. Asking Questions

🎧 Track 038

Listen and Speak!

Questions about the cap

cap

00 : 30

 Key Chunk

| how much | how many | what size | different |

✏️ **Make sentences using the Key Chunk.**

① How much | the cap? | is

② the cap? | What size | is

③ in different colors? | Do you have | the cap

⬇

① How much is the cap?

② _____ is the cap?

③ _____

Your Turn!

🕐 Response Time : 30 seconds

🎤 ①

②

③

Shopping Mall 87

Part 5. Giving Directions

🎧 Track 039

Listen and Speak!

How do you buy the cap for Chris?

shelf

checkout

00 : 30

Key Chunk

stand in the checkout line   look around   pay for   hand over

88   Unit 5

Number the sentences in the correct order.

- ( ) Then, go and stand in the checkout line.
- (1) First, look around the caps on the shelf to find a nice cap.
- ( ) And choose one for Chris.
- ( ) Last, pay for the cap, and the clerk will hand over the wrapped gift.

Your Turn!

Response Time : 30 seconds

Part 6. Retelling a Story

🎧 Track 040

Listen and Speak!

What happened? Where is Julie's coin?

fountain

throw

eagle

00 : 30

✈️ **Key Chunk**

in front of   throw into   took out   fly away

90   Unit 5

✏️ **Fill in the blanks and tell everything that happened.**

Your Turn!

⏰ Response Time : 30 seconds

There was a big fountain _____, and

many people were _____. Julie wanted to

_____ and took out a coin _____. When she threw

it into the fountain, an eagle _____.

The eagle was smiling and _____.

Shopping Mall 91

Presentation

 What do you want to buy at the shopping mall?

SHOPPING LIST

What	Why
①	
②	
③	

✏️ **Write and present your shopping list.**

First, I want to buy
----

because

Unit 5 Word Test

No.	English	Korean
1		
2		
3		
4		
5		
6		
7		
8		
9		
10		

Sentence Practice

Score _____

Unit 6 Science Class

Track 041

Hi! I am Ms. Smith, the science teacher.
Do you like science class?

Science is my favorite subject.
Let's go to the science lab.

Vocabulary Practice

🎧 Track 042
Listen and Repeat!

✏️ Brainstorm and fill in the bubbles.

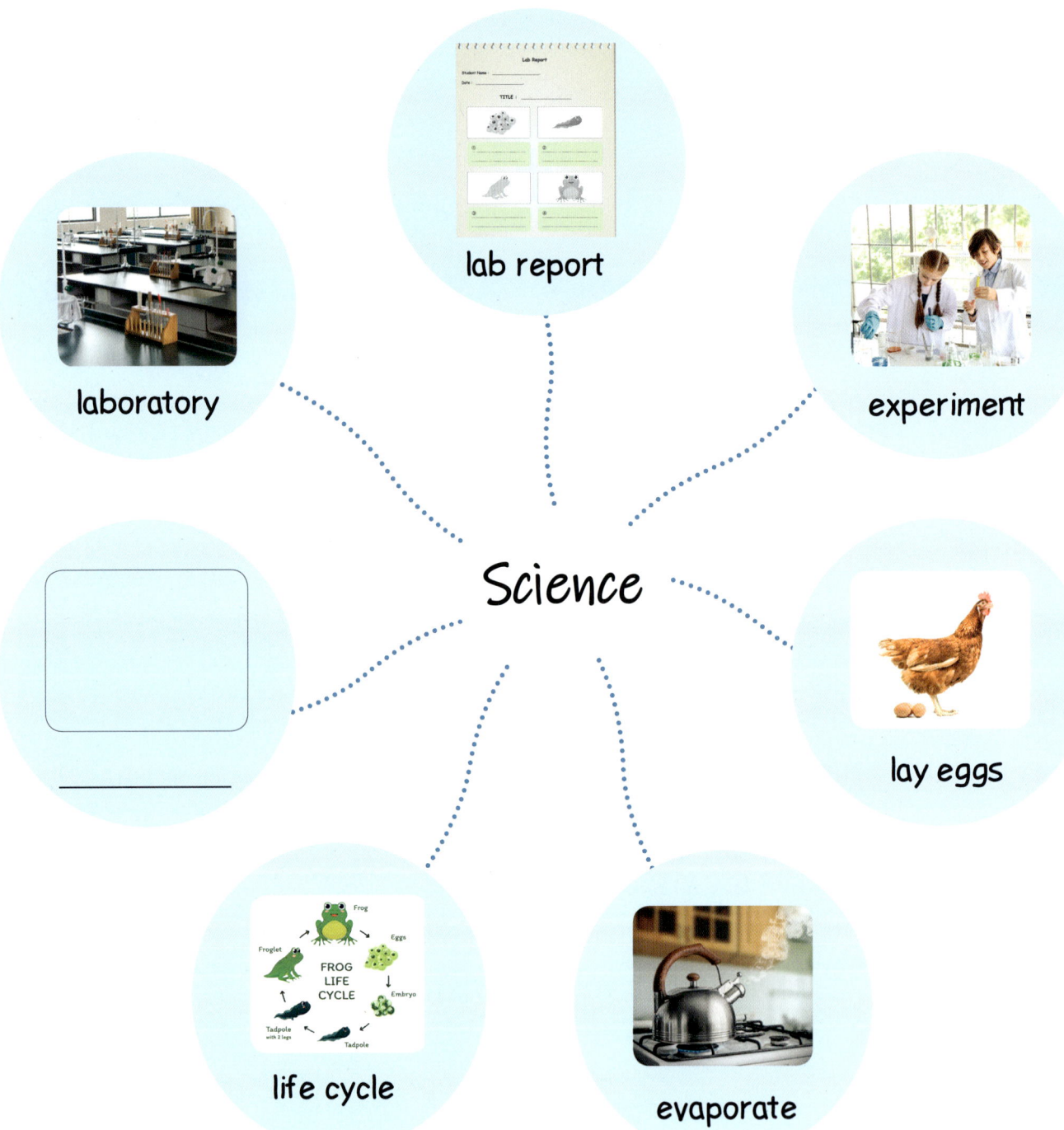

✏️ Fill in the blanks.

1. There is a lot of interesting equipment in the <u>laboratory</u>.

2. Their _____ begins in the spring.

3. The results of the _____ confirmed their study.

4. Hens _____ in the morning.

5. All the water in the pot was _____.

Your Turn!

Science Class

Part 1. Expressing Opinions

🎧 Track 043

Listen and Speak!

What do you like about science class?

00 : 10

✏️ **Fill in the blanks using the Key Chunk.**

- I like science class because I can <u>use</u> a lot of interesting <u>lap equipment</u>.
- I like to _____ in science class.

Your Turn!

⏰ Response Time : 10 seconds

🎤

📎 **Key Chunk**

| learn new things | use lap equipment | favorite subject | interesting field |

98 Unit 6

Part 2. Making Requests

🎧 Track 044

Listen and Speak!

Ask to see the lab equipment.

✏️ **Fill in the blanks using the Key Chunk.**

- Ms. Smith, there is a lot of interesting lab equipment on the shelf . Can I take a look at it?

- Ms. Smith, I w_____ see that lab equipment at the back of the classroom. Can I l_____ ?

Your Turn!

⏰ Response Time : 15 seconds

🎤

Key Chunk

| take a look | there are / is | would like to | look around | on the shelf |

Science Class 99

Part 3. Describing a Picture

Track 045
Listen and Speak!

What is strange in the lab?

Match and complete the sentence.

1. The table is •   • a. smiling.

2. Two chairs are •   • b. swimming in the beaker.

3. Goldfish is •   • c. turtles.

✏️ **Write and tell everything that is strange in the lab using Match and complete the sentence.**

The lab is very strange.

First,

Your Turn!

⏰ Response Time : 20 seconds

Part 4. Asking Questions

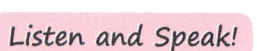 Track 046

Listen and Speak!

Questions about tadpoles

tadpoles

00 : 30

 **Key Chunk**

| what kinds of food | like fish | how small | how big |

✏️ **Make sentences using the Key Chunk.**

① [eat?] [What kinds of food] [do tadpoles]

② [are] [How small] [the tadpoles?]

③ [Do tadpoles] [like fish?] [have gills]

⬇

① What kinds of food do tadpoles eat?

② How small

③

Your Turn!

Response Time : 30 seconds

🎤 ①

②

③

Science Class 103

Part 5. Giving Directions

🎧 Track 047

Listen and Speak!

How do you raise tadpoles?

fish tank

lettuce

tail

00 : 30

Key Chunk

get smaller and smaller   in a few weeks   a little bit of   shady spot

Number the sentences in the correct order.

- ( ) In a few weeks, the eggs will hatch.
- ( ) The tadpoles will grow legs and the tail will get smaller and smaller.
- ( ) After they hatch, feed the tadpoles a little bit of boiled lettuce.
- (1) First, leave the fish tank with frog eggs in a shady spot.

Your Turn!

Response Time : 30 seconds

Science Class

Part 6. Retelling a Story

Listen and Speak!

Track 048

What happened? Where is the popsicle?

popsicle

rock

melt

00 : 30

 **Key Chunk**

become full   on the rock.   run down on   was evaporated

✏️ **Fill in the blanks and tell everything that happened.**

Your Turn!

🎤

⏰ Response Time : 30 seconds

Chris was _____. He became _____ and

wanted to _____. So he put it _____ and

left. It was _____. The popsicle _____

and _____ the rock. Victor licked it. And some of it

_____. Chris came back and _____

because his popsicle _____.

Science Class 107

Presentation

 Look at the frog's life cycle.

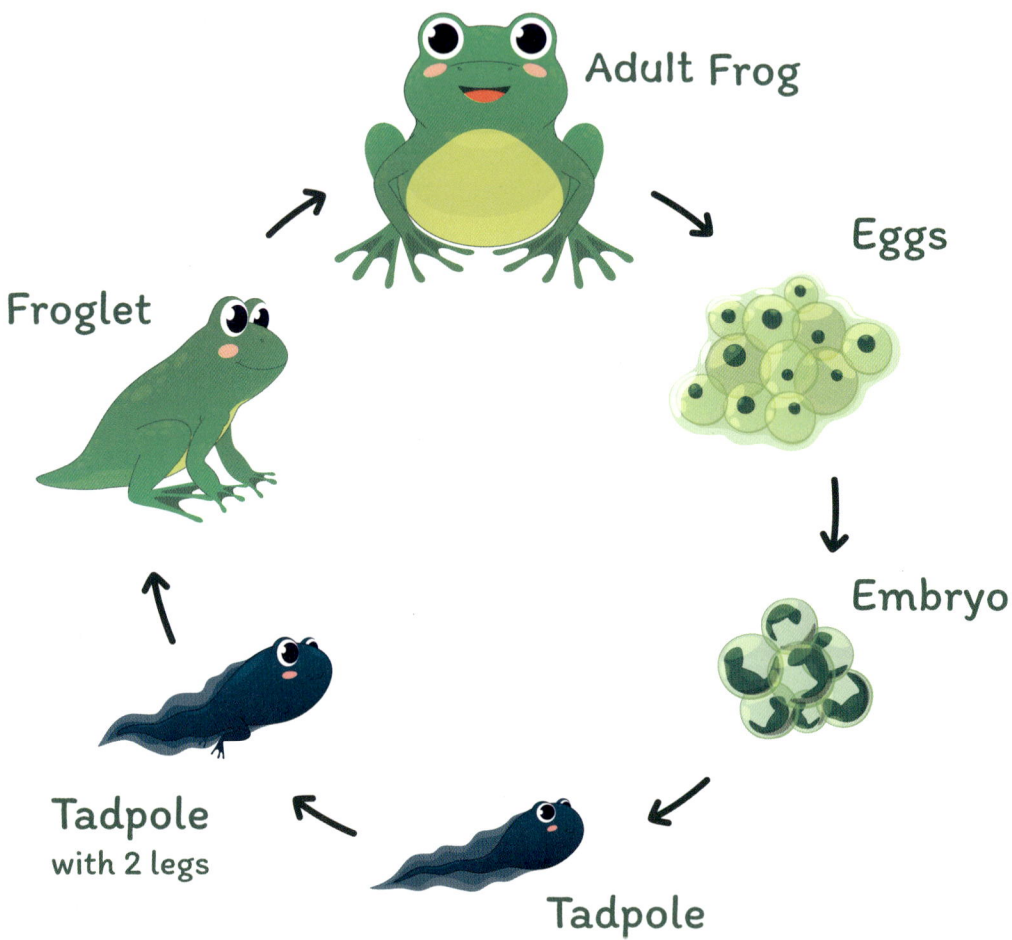

✏️ Write and present your lab report.

Lab Report

Student Name : _____.

Date : _____.

TITLE : _____

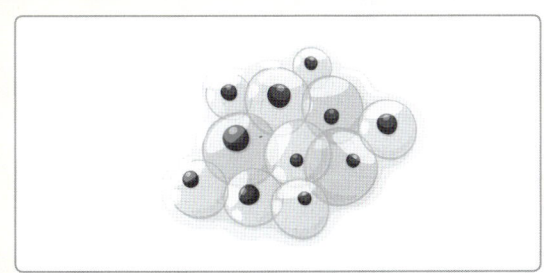

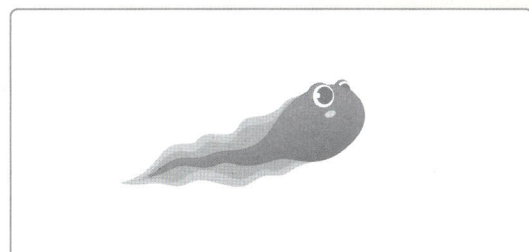

① ------------------------------------- -------------------------------------

② ------------------------------------- -------------------------------------

③ ------------------------------------- -------------------------------------

④ ------------------------------------- -------------------------------------

Science Class

Unit 6 — Word Test

No.	English	Korean
1		
2		
3		
4		
5		
6		
7		
8		
9		
10		

Sentence Practice

Score _____

Actual Test 1

A Mysterious Book in the School Library

Actual Test 1

Track 049-057

SPEAKING
Introduction

Welcome to the school library! Meet Mr. Jones.

SPEAKING
Introduction

Meet friends.

Your Turn!

SPEAKING
Question 2/8

How do you get to the school library?

elevator

shake hands

00 : 30

Your Turn!

SPEAKING
Question 3/8

What is strange in the magazine and newspaper area?

magazine

planet

shelf

00 : 20

Your Turn!

A Mysterious Book in the School Library

SPEAKING
Question 4/8

Ask to borrow a storybook.

00 : 15

Your Turn!

SPEAKING
Question 5/8

How do you borrow a book?

library card

00 : 30

Your Turn!

A Mysterious Book in the School Library 117

SPEAKING
Question 6/8

What happened?

Your Turn!

Your Turn!

SPEAKING
Question 8/8

Which book do you like best? Why?

- comics magazine
- mysterious book
- storybook

00 : 15

Your Turn!

Actual Test 2

Bingo with the Amusement Park Ticket

Actual Test 2

SPEAKING
Introduction

We are going to the amusement park!

SPEAKING
Introduction

Meet friends.

SPEAKING
Question 1/8

What do you like about the amusement park?

00 : 10

Your Turn!

Bingo with the Amusement Park Ticket

SPEAKING
Question 2/8

Questions about the amusement park ticket

00 : 30

Your Turn!

SPEAKING
Question 3/8

What is strange in the animal train?

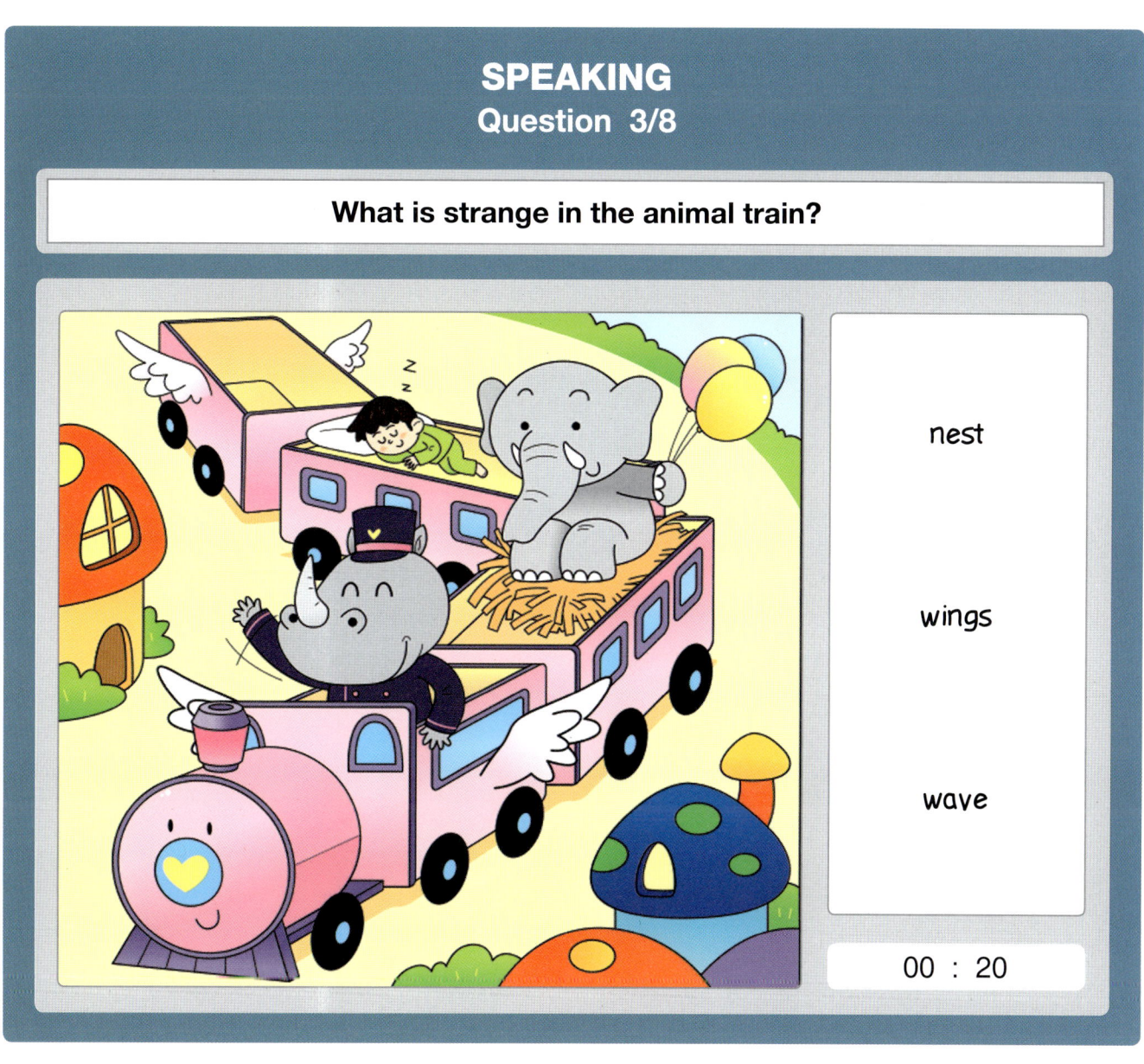

nest

wings

wave

00 : 20

Your Turn!

Bingo with the Amusement Park Ticket

SPEAKING
Question 4/8

What happened?

train station

ticket

wear

00 : 30

Your Turn!

SPEAKING
Question 5/8

How do you ride the Ferris wheel?

Ferris wheel

00 : 30

Your Turn!

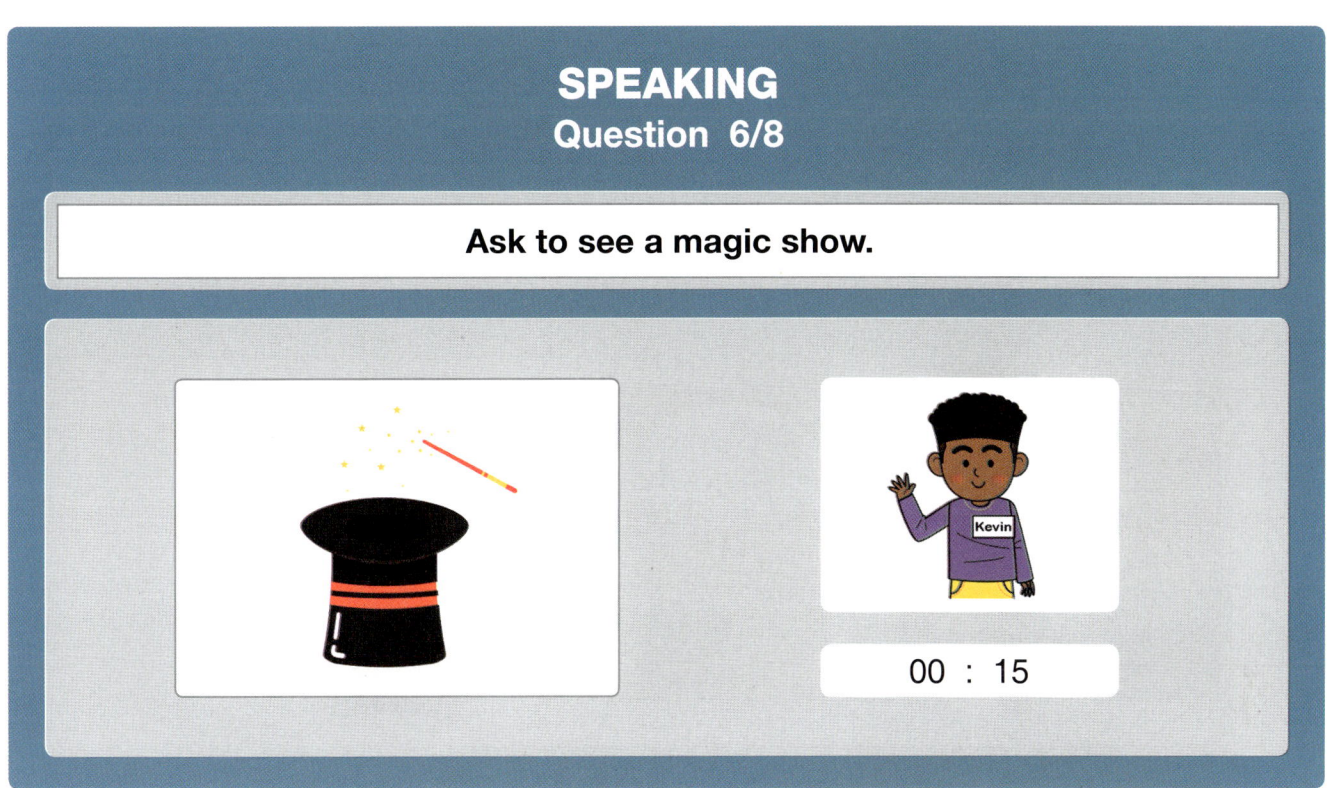

Your Turn!

SPEAKING
Question 7/8

What happened?

stage

magic wand

hold hands

00 : 30

Your Turn!

SPEAKING
Question 8/8

What did you like best in the amusement park? Why did you like it?

00 : 15

Your Turn!

Preparation Book for the TOEFL Primary® Speaking

Answer Key

Preparation Book for the TOEFL Primary® Speaking

Answer Key

Unit 1. House

Chris : Hi! I'm Chris. I want to invite you to my house. Do you want to come after school?
Jack : Hi! I'm Jack. I am going to visit Chris's house with you. Let's go together.
Chris : Welcome to my house. We have lots of things to do today. Let's have fun!

Chris : 안녕! 나는 크리스야. 우리 집에 너를 초대하고 싶어. 학교 끝나고 올래?
Jack : 안녕! 나는 잭이야. 너와 크리스네 집에 갈 거야. 같이 가자.
Chris : 우리 집에 온 걸 환영해. 우리가 오늘 할 게 많이 있어. 재미있게 놀아보자!

Vocabulary Practice
p. 17

> 2. garden   3. living room   4. garage   5. bedroom
>
> *Your Turn!* (Sample Answer)
> I eat breakfast in the kitchen.

Part 1. Expressing Opinions (표현하기)
p. 18

> • watch T.V.
>
> *Your Turn!* (Sample Answer)
> I like to have a snack with my friend because it is more exciting than having a snack alone.

Jack : Do you sometimes visit your friend? We are going to visit Chris's house today. I like to play catch with you and Chris. What do you like to do?

Jack : 너는 가끔 친구 집에 가니? 오늘 우리는 크리스네 집에 갈 거야. 너랑 크리스와 같이 캐치볼을 하고 싶어. 너는 무엇을 하고 싶니?

[해설]

like to ~ : ~하기를 좋아하다, ~하는 것을 좋아하다

- like to 다음에는 동사의 원형을 쓴다.
  I like to sing.   나는 노래하는 것을 좋아한다.
  She likes to read.   그녀는 책읽기를 좋아한다.
  We like to watch TV together.   우리는 함께 TV 보는 것을 좋아한다.

- like to + 동사원형과 like +동사의 -ing는 같은 뜻으로 쓰이므로 바꿔 써도 된다.
  She likes to read. = She likes reading.

Part 2. Making Requests (요청하기)
p. 19

> can you please
>
> *Your Turn!* (Sample Answer)
> I want a glass of water, please.

Jack : We just played catch. It was fun, but we are thirsty. Let's drink some water. But we need to ask Chris first. Ask Chris if we can get some water.

Jack : 우리는 방금 캐치볼 놀이를 했어. 재미있었는데 목이 마르네. 물을 좀 마시자. 하지만 먼저 크리스에게 물어봐야 해. 물을 좀 마실 수 있는지 크리스에게 물어봐.

[해설]

Can you please ~?: ~해줄래요?
- Can you please~?는 ~해달라는 요청이나 부탁의 의미로 쓰이며, please 다음에는 동사의 원형을 쓴다.
  Can you please close the door? 문을 닫아줄래요?
  Can you please answer the phone for me? 나 대신 전화를 받아줄래요?
- 같은 표현으로 Could you~?가 있다.

Part 3. Describing a Picture (설명하기) p. 20~21

1. A cat wearing sunglasses is — c. jumping rope on his bed.
2. His desk is — a. dancing to the music.
3. Books are — b. flying over the bed.

Chris's bedroom is very strange. First, a cat wearing sunglasses is jumping rope on his bed. And his desk is dancing to the music. Books are flying over the bed.

Your Turn! (Sample Answer)
First, there are 2 books flying over his bed, and the door is smiling. A cat is wearing sunglasses and jumping rope on his bed. And his desk is dancing to the music, and the bed is a cheese sandwich.

Jack : Chris has many interesting comic books in his bedroom.
Let's go to his bedroom. First, these words can help you.
I will say a word or a sentence and then you can say it to practice.
jump rope, desk, door
But some things are strange in his bedroom.
For example, a cat wearing sunglasses is jumping rope on Chris's bed.
Many strange things are in his bedroom.
Look at his room again.
Tell me what is strange. Tell me everything that is strange.

Jack : 크리스는 침실에 재미있는 만화책들을 많이 가지고 있대.
크리스의 침실로 가보자.
먼저, 이 단어들이 도움이 될 거야. 내가 단어나 문장을 말한 후에 네가 연습삼아 따라 말하면 돼. / 줄넘기, 책상, 문
그런데 그의 침실에 이상한 것들이 있어. 예를 들면, 선글라스를 쓴 고양이가 크리스의 침대 위에서 줄넘기를 하고 있어.
그의 침실에는 이상한 것들이 많이 있어. 그의 방을 다시 한번 봐.
이상한 것을 얘기해줘. 이상한 것을 모두 말해줘.

Part 4. Asking Questions (질문하기) p. 22~23

① Where do your grandparents live?
② How many siblings do you have?
③ When did your parents get married?

Your Turn! (Sample Answer)
① How tall is your father?
② How old is your mother?
③ Do you have cousins?

Jack : There is a picture of Chris's family. I want to know about his family.
Who is his sister in this picture? How old is she?
What do you want to know about his family?
Tell me three questions you have about his family.

Jack : 크리스네 가족 사진이 있어. 그의 가족에 대해 알고 싶어.
사진에서 크리스의 누나는 누구니? 몇 살이야?
너는 크리스네 가족에 대해 무엇을 알고 싶니?
네가 그의 가족에 대해 알고 싶은 세 가지 질문을 해봐.

Part 5. Giving Directions (지시하기)

p. 24~25

4, 2, 3, 1

Your Turn! (Sample Answer)
First, you need to take the dog food out of the cupboard. And put some dog food into one of the dog bowls. Then, pour some water into the other bowl. Last, call in a loud voice, "Victor! Your lunch is ready!"

Jack : It's time to feed Victor. But first, these words can help you.
I will say a word or a sentence and then you can say it to practice.
cupboard, fridge, dog bowl
Watch what to do.
Chris : I didn't see what to do. Tell me everything I need to do.

Jack : 빅터에게 먹이를 줄 시간이야.
그런데 먼저, 이 단어들이 도움이 될 거야. 내가 단어나 문장을 말한 후에 네가 연습삼아 따라 말하면 돼. / 찬장, 냉장고, 개 밥그릇
무엇을 해야 하는지 봐.
Chris : 난 무엇을 해야 하는 지 못 봤어. 내가 해야 할 일을 전부 말해 줘.

Part 6. Retelling a Story (서술하기)

p. 26~27

Your Turn! (Sample Answer)
Victor was hungry and looking for Chris to ask for food.
First, Victor went to the dining room but no one was there. Then he went to Chris's bedroom. Chris was not there, and his bedroom was very strange. Then he heard Chris calling his name from the kitchen. Victor ran to the kitchen and his dog bow was full of dog food.
Victor was very happy.

Jack : These words can help you.
I will say a word or a sentence and then you can say it to practice.
dining room, bedroom, kitchen
Watch what happens. Watch again.
What happened? What did Victor do? Tell me what Victor did.

Jack : 이 단어들이 도움이 될 거야. 내가 단어나 문장을 말한 후에 네가 연습삼아 따라 말하면 돼. / 식당(식사 방), 침실, 부엌
무슨 일이 일어나는지 지켜봐. 다시 봐.
무슨 일이 벌어졌니? 빅터가 무엇을 했니?
빅터가 했던 일을 말해 줘.

Unit 2. Vacation

Julie : Hi! I'm Julie. It's summer vacation!
Do you like camping? My family is going camping this weekend.
I want to invite you and Jack. Let's go camping together!
Jack : I love camping! Let's go camping.

Julie : 안녕! 나는 줄리야. 여름 방학이다!
너는 캠핑을 좋아하니? 우리 가족은 이번 주말에 캠핑을 가. 너와 잭을 초대하고 싶어. 같이 캠핑 가자!
Jack : 난 캠핑을 아주 좋아해. 함께 캠핑 가자.

Vocabulary Practice

p. 33

2. pack   3. nature   4. relieve   5. beach

Your Turn! (Sample Answer)
I go to the beach to relieve stress.

Part 1. Expressing Opinions (표현하기)
p. 34

- nature
- beach / build a sandcastle

Your Turn! (Sample Answer)
I like to go to the beach with my family because I can play volleyball on the beach.

Jack : It's summer vacation! I am excited!
I like to go camping during vacation.
What do you like to do during vacation?

Jack : 여름 방학이다! 신난다! 방학동안 캠핑을 가고 싶어.
너는 방학동안 무엇을 하고 싶니?

Part 2. Making Requests (요청하기)
p. 35

- this weekend
- going camping / Can I go

Your Turn! (Sample Answer)
Mom, I want to go camping with Julie's family this weekend. Can I?

Jack : I am so excited to go camping with you and Julie's family.
But you need to ask your mom first.
Ask your mom if you can go camping with us.

Jack : 너와 줄리네 가족이랑 같이 캠핑을 가서 난 너무 신나. 하지만 먼저 너의 엄마께 여쭤봐야 해. 우리와 캠핑을 가도 되는지 너의 엄마께 여쭤봐.

> **[해설]**
>
> **Can I ~?: 제가 ~해도 될까요?**
> - Can I ~?는 ~해도 되는지 물어보는 허가나 허락의 의미이며, I 다음에 동사의 원형을 쓴다.
>   Can I use your computer?   당신 컴퓨터를 써도 될까요?
>   Can I play basketball with my friends after school?   학교 끝나고 친구들과 농구를 해도 될까요?
> - 같은 표현으로 May I ~?가 있다.

Part 3. Describing a Picture (설명하기)
p. 36~37

1. There is — a. a big balloon tree in the middle of the boat.
2. The shape of the boat is — b. wearing a captain's hat
3. A bear is — c. a guitar.

(1-c, 2-a, 3-b matching via crossed lines)

The boat is very strange.
First, there is a big balloon tree in the middle of the boat. And the shape of the boat is a guitar. Also, a bear is wearing a captain's hat.

Your Turn! (Sample Answer)
First, the shape of the boat is a guitar and there is a big balloon tree in the middle of the boat. A bear is wearing a captain's hat and a fish is dancing next to the bear. Also, seats are upside down.

Jack : Let's go fishing with Julie's dad. We need to take a boat to cross the lake. First, these words can help you. I will say a word or a sentence and then you can say it to practice.
balloon, fish, captain's hat.
But some things are strange in the boat. For example, there is a big balloon tree in the middle of the boat.
Many strange things are in the boat. Look at the boat again.
Tell me what is strange. Tell me everything that is strange.

Jack : 줄리 아빠와 낚시하러 가자. 호수를 건너려면 배를 타야 해. 먼저, 이 단어들이 도움이 될 거야. 내가 단어나 문장을 말한 후에 네가 연습삼아 따라 말하면 돼. / 풍선, 물고기, 선장 모자
그런데 배 안에 이상한 것들이 있어. 예를 들면, 배 한 가운데에 풍선이 달린 큰 나무가 있어. 배 안에 이상한 것들이 많이 있어. 배를 다시 한 번 봐. 이상한 것을 얘기해줘. 이상한 것을 모두 말해줘.

Part 4. Asking Questions (질문하기)

p. 38~39

① How tall is the tree?
② How old is the tree?
③ What kinds of animals live in the tree?

Your Turn! (Sample Answer)
① How many years does the tree live?
② What kinds of fruits are in the tree?
③ What kinds of birds are living in the tree?

Jack : We are at the campsite. I can see a big tree.
I want to know about the big tree.
How tall is it? What kinds of animals live in the tree?
What do you want to know about it?
Tell me three questions you have about the tree.

Jack : 우리는 캠프장에 와 있어. 큰 나무가 보여. 그 큰 나무에 대해 알고 싶어.
그 나무는 높이가 얼마일까? 어떤 동물들이 그 나무에서 살까? 너는 그 나무에 대해 무엇을 알고 싶니? 네가 그 나무에 대해 알고 싶은 세 가지 질문을 해봐.

Part 5. Giving Directions (지시하기)

p. 40~41

1, 3, 4, 2

Your Turn! (Sample Answer)
First, you need to set up a chair and a fishing rod by the lakeside. Then, cast the fishing rod into the lake as far as you can. Sit down on the chair and wait. Finally, when fish gets caught, strongly pull out the fishing rod.

Jack : Wow! I am excited. I think I can catch lots of fish today.
But first, these words can help you.
I will say a word or a sentence and then you can say it to practice.
fishing rod, chair, lake
Watch what to do.
Julie : I didn't see what to do. Tell me everything I need to do.

Jack : 와! 신난다. 오늘 물고기를 많이 잡을 수 있을 거 같아.
그런데 먼저, 이 단어들이 도움이 될 거야. 내가 단어나 문장을 말한 후에 네가 연습삼아 따라 말하면 돼. / 낚싯대, 의자, 호수
무엇을 해야 하는지 봐.
Julie : 난 무엇을 해야 하는 지 못 봤어. 내가 해야 할 일을 전부 말해 줘.

> **[해설]**
>
> First, Then, Finally: 맨 먼저, 그 다음에, 마지막으로
> - 일의 순서를 나타낼 때 쓰는 표현이다.
>   First, boil some water in a pot. 먼저, 냄비에 물을 끓인다.
>   Next, place the noodles into the pot. 다음, 냄비에 면을 넣는다.
>   Then, add the soup base and vegetable mix and cook for 4 minutes. 그리고 나서, 스프와 야채 믹스를 넣고 4분간 끓인다.
>   Finally, pour the cooked noodles and soup into a bowl and serve. 마지막으로, 조리된 면과 국물을 그릇에 담아 낸다.
> - 순서의 중간에는 second/third, and, also, then, next 등이 쓰이며, 마지막에는 finally, last, lastly, after all 등이 쓰인다.

Part 6. Retelling a Story (서술하기)

Your Turn! (Sample Answer)
Dinner was ready. There were many delicious dishes on the table. But a rabbit appeared and took our fruits. Then a brown bear came. He took our grilled corn and ran away to the forest. Next, a fox came and took our French fries. Last, an eagle flew from the sky and snatched the chicken. The animals took all of our food. Nothing is left and the table is empty now.

Jack : It's time for dinner. These words can help you.
I will say a word or a sentence and then you can say it to practice.
dish, grilled corn, snatch
Watch what happens. Watch again.
What happened? Who took our dinner? Tell me what happened.

Jack : 저녁먹을 시간이야. 이 단어들이 도움이 될 거야. 내가 단어나 문장을 말한 후에 네가 연습삼아 따라 말하면 돼. / 음식, 구운 옥수수, 잡아채다
무슨 일이 일어나는지 지켜봐. 다시 봐.
무슨 일이 벌어졌니? 누가 우리 저녁을 가져갔니? 무슨 일이 벌어졌는지 말해 줘.

Unit 3. Lunch Break

Kevin : Hi! I'm Kevin. It's 12 o'clock. Lunch break!
What do you do during the lunch break?
Jack : I am hungry. Let's go to the cafeteria first!

Kevin : 안녕! 나는 케빈이야. 12시다. 점심시간이다! 점심시간에 넌 무엇을 하니?
Jack : 난 배가 고파. 우선 구내식당으로 가자!

Vocabulary Practice

2. dessert   3. delicious   4. chef   5. awful

Your Turn! (Sample Answer)
She served us an awful dinner.

Part 1. Expressing Opinions (표현하기)

like / best / taste good

Your Turn! (Sample Answer)
I like sushi best because it is healthy food.

Jack : There are many different kinds of food in the cafeteria. I like pasta. Which food do you like?

Jack : 구내식당에는 많은 다양한 종류의 음식이 있어. 나는 파스타를 좋아해. 너는 어떤 음식을 좋아하니?

Part 2. Making Requests (요청하기)
p. 51

- Could you
- get more / favorite dessert

Your Turn! (Sample Answer)
Can you please give me more chocolate cookies? I'd love to get more.

Jack : The lunch was great! Chocolate cookies are my favorite dessert.
Do you want more?
Then ask the cafeteria cook if we can get some more.

Jack : 점심이 아주 맛있었어! 초콜릿 쿠키는 내가 제일 좋아하는 디저트야.
너 좀 더 먹을래? 그러면 우리가 좀 더 먹을 수 있는지 구내식당 요리사에게 물어봐.

Part 3. Describing a Picture (설명하기)
p. 52~53

1. A frog is sleeping — b. on the swings.
2. A rabbit is digging a hole — a. with a shovel.
3. Kids are doing a handstand — c. on a zebra.

The playground is very strange.
First, a frog is sleeping on the swings. And a rabbit is digging a hole with a shovel. Kids are doing a handstand on a zebra.

Your Turn! (Sample Answer)
First, a frog is sleeping on the swings, and a rabbit is digging a hole with a shovel. And kids are doing a handstand on a zebra. Even a bear riding a bike is waving his hand.

Jack : We are full and have some time to play. Let's play in the playground.
First, these words can help you. I will say a word or a sentence and then you can say it to practice.
swings, shovel, handstand
Do you want to play in the playground?
Kevin : Yes, but some things are strange in the playground.
For example, a frog is sleeping on the swings.
Many strange things are in the playground.
Jack : Look at the playground again.
Tell me what is strange. Tell me everything that is strange.

Jack : 우리는 배가 부르고 놀 시간이 있어. 운동장에서 놀자.
먼저, 이 단어들이 도움이 될 거야. 내가 단어나 문장을 말한 후에 네가 연습 삼아 따라 말하면 돼. / 그네, 삽, 물구나무서기
너는 운동장에서 놀고 싶니?

Kevin : 응, 그런데 운동장에 이상한 것들이 있어.
예를 들면, 그네 위에 개구리 한 마리가 자고 있어. 운동장에는 이상한 것들이 많이 있어.
Jack : 운동장을 다시 한번 봐. 이상한 것을 얘기해줘. 이상한 것을 모두 말해줘.

Part 4. Asking Questions (질문하기)
p. 54~55

① How many players are on a basketball team?
② What do you need for playing basketball?
③ How do you get points in basketball?

Your Turn! (Sample Answer)
① How do you prepare before playing basketball?
② How long does a basketball game last?
③ What are the rules of basketball?

Jack : Let's play at the gym. I can see students are playing basketball. Can you play basketball? I want to know about basketball. How many players are on a basketball team? What do you want to know about it? Tell me three questions you have about basketball.	Jack : 체육관에서 놀자. 학생들이 농구를 하고 있는 게 보여. 너 농구할 줄 아니? 난 농구에 대해 알고 싶어. 농구팀에는 몇 명의 선수들이 있니? 너는 농구에 대해 무엇을 알고 싶니? 네가 농구에 대해 알고 싶은 세 가지 질문을 해봐.

[해설]

How many ~ ?: 몇 명의 ~?

- how many 다음에는 셀 수 있는 명사의 복수형이 온다.
  How many students are in a class? 한 반에는 몇 명의 학생들이 있나요?
  How many players are on a soccer team? 축구 팀에는 몇 명의 선수가 있나요?
- how much 다음에는 셀 수 없는 명사가 온다.
  How much money do you have? 너는 돈을 얼마나 가지고 있니?
  How much water is in the vase? 꽃병에는 물이 얼마나 있나요?

Part 5. Giving Directions (지시하기)   p. 56~57

2, 3, 1, 4

Your Turn! (Sample Answer)
Before starting a basketball game, stretch your body first. A basketball game starts at the center of the court when the ball is thrown high up by the referee. Use one hand to bounce the basketball continuously to move the ball. Last, score points by shooting the ball through the hoop.

Kevin : I love basketball. Let me show you how to play basketball. But first, these words can help you. I will say a word or a sentence and then you can say it to practice. referee, bounce, hoop Watch what to do. Jack : I didn't see what to do. Tell me everything I need to do.	Kevin : 난 농구를 아주 좋아해. 농구를 어떻게 하는지 너에게 보여 줄게. 그런데 먼저, 이 단어들이 도움이 될 거야. 내가 단어나 문장을 말한 후에 네가 연습삼아 따라 말하면 돼. / 심판, (공을) 튀기다, (농구의) 링 무엇을 해야 하는지 봐. Jack : 난 무엇을 해야 하는 지 못 봤어. 내가 해야 할 일을 전부 말해 줘.

Part 6. Retelling a Story (서술하기)   p. 58~59

Your Turn! (Sample Answer)
The classroom was empty during the lunch break. Then Max, the school pet, sneaked into the classroom. He ate bananas and drank water on the desk. And then he played in the classroom. He scribbled on the white board and threw things. Soon the classroom was a mess and the school bell rang. Max sneaked out of the classroom.

Kevin : It's time to go back to the classroom. These words can help you. I will say a word or a sentence and then you can say it to practice. white board, mess Watch what happens. Watch again. Jack : What happened? What did Max do? Tell me what happened.	Kevin : 교실로 돌아갈 시간이야. 이 단어들이 도움이 될 거야. 내가 단어나 문장을 말한 후에 네가 연습삼아 따라 말하면 돼. / 흰색 칠판, 난장판 무슨 일이 일어나는지 지켜봐. 다시 봐. Jack : 무슨 일이 벌어졌니? 맥스가 무슨 일을 했니? 무슨 일이 생겼는지 말해 줘.

Unit 4. Field Trip

Ms. Perry : Hi! I'm the art teacher, Ms. Perry. We are going on a field trip.
Where do you want to go?
Jack : I like paintings! I want to go to an art museum.
Do you want to come with us?

Ms. Perry : 안녕! 나는 미술을 가르치는 페리선생님이야. 우리는 현장학습을 갈 거야. 너희들은 어디로 가고 싶니?
Jack : 저는 그림을 좋아해요! 저는 미술관에 가고 싶어요. 너도 우리와 같이 갈래?

Vocabulary Practice
p. 65

2. educational   3. art museum   4. purpose   5. itinerary

Your Turn! (Sample Answer)
Going on a field trip can be very fun.

Part 1. Expressing Opinions (표현하기)
p. 66

• hanging out

Your Turn! (Sample Answer)
I like to experience new things on a field trip.

Ms. Perry : We are going on a field trip next week. I am excited!
I like visiting interesting places on the field trip.
What do you like about field trips?

Ms. Perry : 다음 주에 현장학습을 갈 거예요. 신이 나네요!
선생님은 현장학습으로 흥미로운 장소들을 방문하는 것을 좋아해요. 너는 현장학습의 어떤 점을 좋아하니?

> **[해설]**
>
> **What do you like about ~? ~의 무엇이 좋니?**
>
> • What do you like about ~?은 ~의 어떤 점을 좋아하는지를 묻는 질문이다.
> What do you like about Korea? / I like the food, the people, and the atmosphere.
> What do you like about your best friend? / When I call her in need, she will be there for me.

Part 2. Making Requests (요청하기)
p. 67

• could you / learn about

Your Turn! (Sample Answer)
Ms. Perry, could you take us to an art museum for a field trip? We want to learn about famous paintings.

Jack : I like art. I want to go to an art museum for a field trip.
How about you? Where do you want to go for a field trip?
Let's ask Ms. Perry if we can go on a field trip to where we want to go.

Jack : 저는 미술을 좋아해요. 현장학습으로 미술관에 가면 좋겠어요. 너는 어때?
너는 현장학습으로 어디를 가고 싶니? 우리가 가고 싶은 곳으로 현장학습을 가도 되는지 페리 선생님께 여쭤보자.

Part 3. Describing a Picture (설명하기)　　　　　　　　　　　　　　　　　　p. 68~69

1. Frogs are　　　　•　　　　　　　　　•　a. looking at the paintings.
2. The Thinker is　•　　　　　　　　　•　b. sitting on the nest.
3. The ceiling lights are　•　　　　　•　c. oranges.

European Art room is very strange.
First, frogs are looking at the paintings. And the Thinker is sitting on the nest. The ceiling lights are oranges.

Your Turn! (Sample Answer)
First, frogs are looking at the paintings. The Thinker is sitting on the nest. And Mona Lisa is wearing a crown. Even the ceiling lights are oranges.

Jack	: I want to see European Art. First, these words can help you. I will say a word or a sentence and then you can say it to practice. bench, nest, crown Do you want to see European Art with me?	Jack	: 난 유럽 미술을 보고 싶어. 먼저, 이 단어들이 도움이 될 거야. 내가 단어나 문장을 말한 후에 네가 연습 삼아 따라 말하면 돼. / 긴 의자, 둥지, 왕관 나와 함께 유럽 미술을 보고 싶니?
Ms. Perry	: But some things are strange in the European Art room. For example, Mona Lisa is wearing a crown. There are many strange things in the European Art room.	Ms. Perry	: 그런데 유럽 미술실에 이상한 것들이 있네요. 예를 들면, 모나리자가 왕관을 쓰고 있어요. 유럽 미술실에 이상한 것들이 많이 있네요.
Jack	: Look at the art room again. Tell me what is strange. Tell me everything that is strange.	Jack	: 미술실을 다시 한 번 봐. 이상한 것을 얘기해줘. 이상한 것을 모두 말해줘.

[해설]

is made of~ : ~로 만들어진

- be made of는 재료가 물건으로 만들어진 후에도 그 재료의 기본 형태가 변하지 않는 경우에 사용한다.
  The chair is made of wood.
  The Hanbok is made of silk.

- be made from은 재료가 물건으로 만들어진 후에는 그 재료의 형태가 사라진 경우에 사용한다.
  This ice cream is made from milk.
  Wine is made from grapes.

Part 4. Asking Questions (질문하기)　　　　　　　　　　　　　　　　　　p. 70~71

① Where did this vase come from?
② What was this vase used for?
③ What is this vase made of?

Your Turn! (Sample Answer)
① How old is this vase?
② Does this vase come from China?
③ Who found this vase?

| Jack | : | We are at the art museum. There is beautiful vase in the lobby.
I want to know about the vase and where it is from.
What do you want to know about it?
Tell me three questions you have about the vase. | Jack | 우리는 미술관에 와 있어. 로비에 아름다운 꽃병이 있어.
나는 그 꽃병과 그게 어디에서 왔는지 알고 싶어.
너는 꽃병에 대해 무엇을 알고 싶니?
네가 꽃병에 대해 알고 싶은 세가지 질문을 해봐. |
|---|---|---|---|---|

Part 5. Giving Directions (지시하기)

p. 72~73

4, 1, 2, 3

Your Turn! (Sample Answer)
First, listen to Ms. Perry carefully while she explains how to complete the worksheet. Then, we need to prepare a pencil and line up in front of her. When we receive the worksheet, we should write down our name on it. Last, we can look around in the museum and complete the worksheet.

| Ms. Perry | : | You need to complete the worksheet during the field trip.
But first, these words can help you. I will say a word or a sentence and then you can say it to practice.
worksheet, in front of
Watch what to do. | Ms. Perry | 현장학습 동안 평가지를 완성해야 해요.
그런데 먼저, 이 단어들이 도움이 될 거예요. 선생님이 단어나 문장을 말한 후에 여러분은 연습삼아 따라 말하면 돼요. / 평가지, ~ 앞에
무엇을 해야 하는지 보세요. |
|---|---|---|---|---|
| Jack | : | I didn't see what to do. Tell me everything I need to do. | Jack | 난 무엇을 해야 하는 지 못 봤어. 내가 해야 할 일을 전부 말해 줘. |

Part 6. Retelling a Story (서술하기)

p. 74~75

Your Turn! (Sample Answer)
Max had lots of treats in his hands. He wanted to hide them and was looking for some places. He climbed up the tree in the garden and hid some lollipops. Then, he hid some chocolates under the tree and covered them with leaves and branches. Next, he drew a treasure map and gave it to Ms. Perry.

| Ms. Perry | : | Max gave me this map. I think it is a treasure map.
What did Max hide? These words can help you.
I will say a word or a sentence and then you can say it to practice.
hide, lollipop, branch
Watch what happens. Watch again. | Ms. Perry | 맥스가 선생님에게 이 지도를 줬어요. 보물지도 같아요.
맥스는 무엇을 숨겼을까요?
이 단어들이 도움이 될 거예요. 선생님이 단어나 문장을 말한 후에 여러분이 연습삼아 따라 말하면 돼요. / 숨기다, 막대 사탕, 나뭇가지
무슨 일이 일어나는지 지켜보세요. 다시 보세요. |
|---|---|---|---|---|
| Jack | : | What happened? What did Max do? Tell me what happened. | Jack | 무슨 일이 벌어졌니? 맥스가 무엇을 했니? 무슨 일이 생겼는지 말해 줘. |

Unit 5. Shopping Mall

| Julie | : | Hi! I love shopping. Do you like shopping?
What do you buy at the mall?
I am going to the mall to buy Chris's birthday gift this weekend. Do you want to come? | Julie | 안녕! 난 쇼핑을 아주 좋아해. 넌 쇼핑 좋아하니?
넌 쇼핑몰에서 무엇을 사니? 난 이번 주말에 크리스의 생일 선물을 사러 쇼핑몰에 갈 거야. 너도 갈래? |
|---|---|---|---|---|
| Jack | : | I like shopping! Let's go to the mall. | Jack | 나는 쇼핑을 좋아해. 같이 쇼핑몰로 가자. |

Vocabulary Practice
p. 81

2. window shopping   3. hang out   4. store   5. downtown

Your Turn! (Sample Answer)
I will hang out with my friends tomorrow.

Part 1. Expressing Opinions (표현하기)
p. 82

• hanging out / spend time

Your Turn! (Sample Answer)
I like spending time in the shopping mall because I like to see different kinds of clothing shops.

Julie : I like hanging out with my friends at the shopping mall.
There are many interesting places.
What do you like about the mall?

Julie : 난 쇼핑몰에서 친구들과 놀며 시간을 보내는 것을 좋아해.
흥미로운 장소들이 많이 있어. 너는 쇼핑몰의 어떤 점이 좋니?

Part 2. Making Requests (요청하기)
p. 83

• coming up / present for him

Your Turn! (Sample Answer)
Mom, I need to buy a birthday gift for Chris. Can I go to the mall with Julie?

Jack : Let's go to the shopping mall. We need to buy Chris's birthday gift.
But you need to ask your mom first.
Ask your mom if you can go to the mall with us.

Jack : 같이 쇼핑몰에 가자. 우리는 크리스의 생일 선물을 사야 해.
하지만 먼저 너의 엄마께 여쭤봐야 해. 우리와 쇼핑몰에 가도 되는지 너의 엄마께 여쭤봐.

Part 3. Describing a Picture (설명하기)
p. 84~85

1. A giraffe is — b. trying on high heels.
2. Handstanding kids are — a. wearing shoes on their hands.
3. Shoes are — c. flying around.

The shoe store is very strange.
First, a giraffe is trying on high heels. And the handstanding kids are wearing shoes on their hands. Shoes are flying around.

Your Turn! (Sample Answer)
First, a giraffe is trying on high heels. And the handstanding kids are wearing shoes on their hands. Shoes are flying around. Even the mirror is smiling.

Julie : How about shoes for Chris's birthday gift? Let's go to the shoe store. First, these words can help you. I will say a word or a sentence and then you can say it to practice.
mirror, giraffe, handstand

Jack : But some things are strange in the shoe store.
For example, a giraffe is trying on high heels.
Many strange things are in the shoe store.

Julie : Look at the shoe store again.
Tell me what is strange. Tell me everything that is strange.

Julie : 크리스의 생일 선물로 신발은 어떨까? 신발 가게로 가 보자. 먼저, 이 단어들이 도움이 될 거야. 내가 단어나 문장을 말한 후에 네가 연습 삼아 따라 말하면 돼. / 거울, 기린, 물구나무서기를 하다.

Jack : 그런데 신발 가게에 이상한 것들이 있어.
예를 들면, 기린이 굽 높은 신발을 신어보고 있어. 신발 가게에는 이상한 것들이 많이 있어.

Julie : 신발 가게를 다시 한 번 봐.
이상한 것을 얘기해줘. 이상한 것을 모두 말해줘.

[해설]

try on ~: ~을 입어보다, 신어보다
- try on은 옷, 모자, 신발 따위를 한 번 착용해보다의 의미로 쓰인다.
  You should try on the dress to see if it fits. 그 드레스가 잘 맞는지 입어봐야 한다.
  Try on these gloves. 이 장갑을 한 번 껴봐.

Part 4. Asking Questions (질문하기)   p. 86~87

① How much is the cap?
② What size is the cap?
③ Do you have the cap in different colors?

Your Turn! (Sample Answer)
① What material is this cap made of?
② How many caps are left in stock?
③ Do you have the bigger size of this cap?

Julie : Let's go to the hat store.
I think this cap is perfect for Chris. I want to know what size it is. What do you want to know about this cap? Tell me three questions you have about the cap.

Julie : 모자 가게로 가 보자.
크리스에게 이 모자가 잘 어울릴 거 같아. 이 모자는 사이즈가 몇인지 알고 싶어. 너는 이 모자에 대해 무엇을 알고 싶니? 네가 이 모자에 대해 알고 싶은 세 가지 질문을 해봐.

Part 5. Giving Directions (지시하기)   p. 88~89

3, 1, 2, 4

Your Turn! (Sample Answer)
First, look around the caps on the shelf to find a nice cap. And choose one for Chris. Then go and stand in the checkout line. Last, pay for the cap, and the clerk will hand over the wrapped gift.

Julie : How can we buy a cap?
First, these words can help you. I will say a word or a sentence and then you can say it to practice.
shelf, checkout
Watch what to do.
Jack : I didn't see what to do. Tell me everything I need to do.

Julie : 모자는 어떻게 살 수 있지?
그런데 먼저, 이 단어들이 도움이 될 거야. 내가 단어나 문장을 말한 후에 네가 연습삼아 따라 말하면 돼. / 선반, 계산대
무엇을 해야 하는지 봐.
Jack : 난 무엇을 해야 하는 지 못 봤어. 내가 해야 할 일을 전부 말해 줘.

Part 6. Retelling a Story (서술하기)   p. 90~91

Your Turn! (Sample Answer)
There was a big fountain in front of the shopping mall, and many people were throwing coins into it. Julie wanted to try it and took out a coin from her purse. When she threw it into the fountain, an eagle flew to Julie and snatched her coin. The eagle was smiling and flying away with the coin.

| Jack | : | There is a beautiful wishing fountain in front of the mall. Many people are throwing coins into it. These words can help you.
I will say a word or a sentence and then you can say it to practice.
fountain, throw, eagle
Watch what happens. Watch again.

What happened? What happened to Julie? Tell me what happened. | Jack | : | 쇼핑몰 앞에 아름다운 소원분수가 있어.
많은 사람들이 그 안으로 동전을 던지고 있어.
이 단어들이 도움이 될 거야. 내가 단어나 문장을 말한 후에 네가 연습삼아 따라 말하면 돼. / 분수, 던지다, 독수리
무슨 일이 일어나는지 지켜봐. 다시 봐.

무슨 일이 벌어졌니? 줄리에게 무슨 일이 생겼어? 무슨 일이 벌어졌는지 말해 줘. |

Unit 6. Science Class

| Ms. Smith | : | Hi! I am Ms. Smith, and I'm a science teacher.
Do you like science class? | Ms. Smith | : | 안녕! 나는 스미스 선생님이고, 과학을 가르쳐요.
너는 과학 수업을 좋아하니? |
| Jack | : | Science is my favorite subject. Let's go to the science lab! | Jack | : | 과학은 제가 제일 좋아하는 과목이에요. 과학실로 가요! |

Vocabulary Practice   p. 97

2. life cycle   3. experiment   4. lay eggs   5. evaporated

Your Turn! (Sample Answer)
The lab report is important for keeping a record of the research.

Part 1. Expressing Opinions (표현하기)   p. 98

• learn new things

Your Turn! (Sample Answer)
I like science class because science is an interesting field.

| Ms. Smith | : | Do you like science class?
I like science class because I can use interesting lab equipment.
What do you like about science class? | Ms. Smith | : | 너는 과학 수업을 좋아하니?
선생님은 흥미로운 실험 장비들을 사용할 수 있어서 과학 수업을 좋아한단다. 너는 과학 수업의 어떤 점을 좋아하니? |

[해설]

a lot of ~: 많은 ~

- a lot of는 셀 수 있는 명사 또는 셀 수 없는 명사와 함께 사용할 수 있고, 수와 양이 많음을 나타낸다.
  I have a lot of friends. 나는 친구가 많다.
  The teacher gave us a lot of homework. 선생님께서 우리에게 많은 숙제를 내주셨다.
- 같은 표현으로 쓰이는 lots of도 셀 수 있는 명사 또는 셀 수 없는 명사와 함께 사용할 수 있다.

Part 2. Making Requests (요청하기)

p. 99

- would like to / look around

Your Turn! (Sample Answer)
Ms. Smith, would you mind if I see those lab equipment on the shelf?

Jack : There is a lot of interesting lab equipment in the science lab. Do you want to take a look at it?
Ask Ms. Smith if you can take a look at the lab equipment.

Jack : 과학실에는 흥미로운 실험 장비들이 많이 있어. 한 번 볼래? 실험 장비를 봐도 되는지 스미스 선생님께 여쭤 봐.

[해설]

would like to~: ~했으면 좋겠다, ~하고 싶다

- would like to는 like to나 want to 보다 공손한 표현이다. To 다음에는 동사의 원형이 온다.
  I would like to be friends with you.   나는 너와 친구가 됐으면 좋겠어요.
  I'd like to reserve a room for Sunday.   일요일에 사용할 방을 예약하고 싶어요.

Part 3. Describing a Picture (설명하기)

p. 100~101

1. The table is   •   •   a. smiling.
2. Two chairs are   •   •   b. swimming in the beaker.
3. Goldfish is   •   •   c. turtles.

The lab is very strange.
First, the table is smiling. And two chairs are turtles. Goldfish is swimming in the beaker.

Your Turn! (Sample Answer)
First, the table is smiling and two chairs are turtles. Goldfish is swimming in the beaker. Even the microscope is upside down.

Ms. Smith : It's time to start the class. Please sit around the lab table.
First, these words can help you. I will say a word or a sentence and then you can say it to practice.
microscope, goldfish, turtle

Jack : But some things are strange in our lab.
For example, the table is smiling.
Many strange things are in the lab.

Ms. Smith : Look at the lab again.
Tell me what is strange. Tell me everything that is strange.

Ms. Smith : 수업을 시작할 시간이예요. 실험 탁자에 둘러 앉으세요.
먼저, 이 단어들이 도움이 될 거예요. 선생님이 단어나 문장을 말한 후에 여러분이 연습삼아 따라 말하면 돼요. / 현미경, 금붕어, 거북이

Jack : 그런데 우리 실험실에 이상한 것들이 있어요.
예를 들면, 탁자가 웃고 있어요. 실험실에 이상한 것들이 많이 있어요.

Ms. Smith : 실험실을 다시 한 번 보세요.
이상한 것을 얘기해 보세요. 이상한 것을 모두 말해 보세요.

Part 4. Asking Questions (질문하기) p. 102~103

① What kinds of food do tadpoles eat?
② How small are the tadpoles?
③ Do tadpoles have gills like fish?

Your Turn! (Sample Answer)
① How big are the tadpoles?
② What kinds of food do tadpoles not like?
③ How big are the tadpoles after they grow?

Jack : We are learning about a frog's life cycle today. Do you know about tadpoles? I want to know how small they are. What do you want to know about them? Tell me three questions you have about tadpoles.

Jack : 오늘 우리는 개구리의 생애 주기에 대해서 배워. 너는 올챙이에 대해 아니? 난 올챙이가 얼마나 작은 지 알고 싶어. 너는 올챙이에 대해 무엇을 알고 싶니? 네가 올챙이에 대해 알고 싶은 세가지 질문을 해봐.

Part 5. Giving Directions (지시하기) p. 104~105

2, 4, 3, 1

Your Turn! (Sample Answer)
First, leave the fish tank with frog eggs in a shady spot. In a few weeks, the eggs will hatch. After they hatch, feed the tadpoles a little bit of boiled lettuce. The tadpoles will grow legs and the tail will get smaller and smaller.

Ms. Smith : We will raise tadpoles during this semester.
Let me teach you how to raise tadpoles. These words can help you.
I will say a word or a sentence and then you can say it to practice.
fish tank, lettuce, tail

Ms. Smith : Let me teach you how to raise tadpoles. Watch what to do.

Jack : I want to raise tadpoles but I didn't see what to do. Tell me everything I need to do.

Ms. Smith : 이번 학기동안 올챙이를 길러 볼 거예요. 올챙이 기르는 방법을 알려 줄게요.
이 단어들이 도움이 될 거예요. 선생님이 단어나 문장을 말한 후에 여러분은 연습삼아 따라 말하면 돼요. / 어항, 상추, 꼬리

Ms. Smith : 올챙이 기르는 방법을 알려 줄게요. 무엇을 해야 하는 지 보세요.

Jack : 난 올챙이를 키우고 싶은데 무엇을 해야 하는 지 못 봤어. 내가 해야 할 일을 전부 말해 줘.

Part 6. Retelling a Story (서술하기) p. 106~107

Your Turn! (Sample Answer)
Chris was eating a popsicle. He became full and wanted to eat the rest later. So he put it on the rock and left. It was sunny and hot. The popsicle started to melt and ran down on the rock. Victor licked it. And some of it was evaporated. Chris came back and was surprised because his popsicle disappeared.

Jack : It is hot. Chris wants to eat the popsicle. Where is the popsicle?
These words can help you. I will say a word or a sentence and then you can say it to practice.
popsicle, rock, melt
Watch what happens. Watch again.

What happened? What happened to Chris's popsicle? Tell me what happened.

Jack : 덥다. 크리스는 남겨둔 아이스캔디를 먹고 싶대. 아이스캔디는 어디 있지?
이 단어들이 도움이 될 거야. 내가 단어나 문장을 말한 후에 네가 연습 삼아 따라 말하면 돼. / 아이스캔디, 바위, 녹다
무슨 일이 일어나는지 지켜봐. 다시 봐.

무슨 일이 벌어졌니? 크리스의 아이스캔디에 무슨 일이 생겼니? 무슨 일이 벌어졌는지 말해 줘.

Actual Test 1. A Mysterious Book in the School Library

Mr. Jones : Hello, my name is Mr. Jones. I am a school librarian. And these are my students Julie and Chris. Our school library has many books, magazines, newspapers, and a mysterious book! Today, we are going to look around the school library and find the mysterious book.

Julie : Hi ~ I'm Julie. I am going to the school library with you.

Chris : Hi ~ I'm Chris. I am also looking for the mysterious book with you.

Mr. Jones : 안녕, 나는 존스 선생님이예요. 학교 도서관 사서예요. 여기는 나의 학생인 줄리와 크리스예요. 우리 학교 도서관에는 많은 책, 잡지, 신문 그리고 신비로운 책이 한 권 있어요. 오늘 우리는 학교 도서관을 둘러보면서 그 신비의 책을 찾아볼 거예요.

Julie : 안녕~ 난 줄리야. 너와 함께 학교 도서관에 갈 거야.

Chris : 안녕~ 난 크리스야. 나도 너와 함께 신비의 책을 찾아볼 거야.

Question 1
p. 113

> **Your Turn!** (Sample Answer)
> I like reading new books in the library.

Mr. Jones : We are going to look around the school library today.
There are many interesting things in the library. I like old newspapers. What do you like about the library?
We are going to see many interesting things today.

Mr. Jones : 우리는 오늘 학교 도서관을 둘러볼 거예요.
도서관에는 흥미로운 것들이 많이 있어요. 선생님은 오래된 신문을 좋아해요. 여러분은 도서관의 어떤 점을 좋아하나요?
오늘 우리는 많은 재미있는 것들을 보게 될 거예요.

Question 2
p. 114

> **Your Turn!** (Sample Answer)
> First, I follow the sign. And I shake hands with the elevator.
> I get into the elevator and press 5. I get out and wave goodbye to the elevator.

Julie : These words can help you. Elevator, shake hands.
Let's go to the school library. Watch what to do.

Chris : I didn't see what to do. How do you get to the school library?
Tell me everything I need to do.
Thanks! Let's go to the magazine and newspaper area first. I will meet you there soon.

Julie : 이 단어들이 도움이 될 거야. / 엘리베이터, 악수하다
학교 도서관으로 가자. 무엇을 해야 하는지 봐.

Chris : 난 무엇을 해야 하는 지 못 봤어. 도서관으로 가려면 어떻게 해야 하지?
내가 해야 할 일을 전부 말해 줘.
고마워! 우선 잡지와 신문 구역으로 가 보자. 곧 거기서 만나.

> **[해설]**
>
> **How do you get to 장소? 장소까지 어떻게 가나요?**
> - Get to 다음에 장소가 오면 그 장소에 도착하다의 뜻을 가진다.
>   Generally, I get to school at 8:30am.　보통 나는 오전 8시 30분에 학교에 도착한다.
>   We got to Qatar that evening.　우리는 그 날 저녁에 카타르에 도착했다.

Question 3
p. 115

> **Your Turn!** (Sample Answer)
> First, a turtle is looking at a magazine. And a shelf is dancing. The boy is holding a book upside down.

Mr. Jones : These words can help you.
I will say a word or a sentence and then you can say it to practice.
magazine, planet, shelf.
Julie : Some strange things are in the magazine and newspaper area. For example, a turtle wearing glasses is reading a magazine. Many strange things are in the magazine and newspaper area. That is strange. Look at the magazine and newspaper area again. Tell me what is strange. Tell me everything that is strange.
Wow! It is very strange.

Mr. Jones : 이 단어들이 도움이 될 거예요.
선생님이 단어나 문장을 말한 후에 여러분은 연습삼아 따라 말하면 돼요. / 잡지, 행성, 선반
Julie : 잡지와 신문 구역에 이상한 것들이 있어요. 예를 들면, 안경을 쓴 거북이가 잡지를 읽고 있어요. 잡지와 신문 구역에 이상한 것들이 많이 있어요. 이상해요. 잡지와 신문 구역을 다시 한 번 보세요. 이상한 것을 얘기해줘. 이상한 것을 모두 말해줘.
와! 매우 이상하다.

Question 4
p. 116

> **Your Turn!** (Sample Answer)
> I'd like to borrow a storybook, please.

Julie : I think the mysterious book is a storybook.
Let's borrow a storybook. We need to ask the librarian first.
Ask the librarian if we can borrow a storybook.
Mr. Jones : Sure! Let me show you how to borrow a book.

Julie : 내 생각에 그 신비한 책은 이야기 책인 거 같아.
이야기 책을 한 권 빌려보자. 우선 사서선생님께 여쭤봐야 해. 우리가 이야기 책을 빌릴 수 있는지 사서선생님께 여쭤봐.
Mr. Jones : 물론이에요! 책을 대여하는 방법을 보여 줄게요.

Question 5
p. 117

> **Your Turn!** (Sample Answer)
> First, look at the books on the shelf. Then choose a book. Next, give the book and your library card to the librarian. Finally, check the return date and take the book and your library card back.

Mr. Jones : These words can help you: Library card.
Don't forget your library card. Watch what to do.
Chris : I didn't see what to do. How do I borrow a book?
Tell me everything I need to do.
Thanks. I am going to borrow a storybook.
I think the mysterious book is a storybook.

Mr. Jones : 이 단어들이 도움이 될 거에요: 대출증
대출증을 잊지 마세요. 무엇을 해야 하는지 보세요.
Chris : 난 무엇을 해야 하는 지 못 봤어. 책을 어떻게 대출하니?
내가 해야 할 일을 전부 말해 줘.
고마워. 나는 이야기 책을 한 권 대출할 거야. 그 신비한 책이 이야기 책인 거 같거든.

Question 6
p. 118~119

> **Your Turn!** (Sample Answer)
> First, Chris was looking at the books, and one of them was shiny and mysterious. He picked it up. When he opened it, a whirlwind started inside it. The main characters in the story appeared. They said hello to Chris, and he was surprised. Chris closed the book.

| Mr. Jones | : | These words can help you: Shiny, mysterious book, whirlwind.
Watch what happens in the storybook area. Watch again.
What happened? What did Chris do? Tell me what Chris did.
Thank you. | Mr. Jones | : | 이 단어들이 도움이 될 거예요: 빛나는, 신비한 책, 회오리 바람
이야기책 구역에서 무슨 일이 벌어지는지 지켜보세요. 다시 보세요.
무슨 일이 벌어졌나요? 크리스가 무엇을 했나요? 크리스가 한 일을 말해보세요.
고마워요. |
|---|---|---|---|---|---|

Question 7

p. 120

> **Your Turn!** (Sample Answer)
> Who wrote the mysterious book?
> Is the book real?
> Where can I find a book like that?

| Mr. Jones | : | It was a great day! We found the mysterious book.
I have a lot of questions about the mysterious book, like who wrote it.
What questions do you have about the mysterious book?
Tell me three questions you have about the mysterious book.
Those are good questions. | Mr. Jones | : | 멋진 날이었어요. 우리는 그 신비한 책을 찾았어요.
선생님은 그 신비한 책을 누가 썼는 지와 같이 그 책에 대해 궁금한 것이 많아요.
너는 그 신비한 책에 대해 무엇을 알고 싶니? 네가 그 신비한 책에 대해 알고 싶은 세 가지 질문을 해보세요.
좋은 질문이에요. |
|---|---|---|---|---|---|

Question 8

p. 121

> **Your Turn!** (Sample Answer)
> I like the comics magazine best. I like the colorful pictures. And I enjoy exciting stories about amazing people.

Chris	:	Yeah! We found the mysterious book!	Chris	:	와! 우리가 그 신비한 책을 찾았어!
Mr. Jones	:	We had a lot of fun today and chances to see many different kinds of books like magazines and storybooks. Which book did you like best?	Mr. Jones	:	오늘 아주 재미있었고 잡지와 이야기책과 같은 많은 다양한 종류의 책들을 볼 기회를 가졌어요. 여러분은 어떤 책이 가장 좋았어요?
Chris	:	I liked the mysterious book best. It was so amazing. I met many interesting storybook characters. Which book do you like best? And why?	Chris	:	저는 신비한 책이 제일 좋았어요. 아주 놀라웠어요.
저는 흥미로운 이야기책 등장인물들을 많이 만났어요.
너는 어떤 책을 가장 좋아하니? 그 이유는 무엇이니?
Mr. Jones	:	Thank you for visiting our school library. I hope to see you again. Bye!	Mr. Jones	:	우리 학교 도서관을 방문해줘서 고마워요. 다시 만날 수 있기를 바래요. 잘 가요!

> **[해설]**
>
> **Which ~ do you like best? 너는 어떤 ~을 제일 좋아하니?**
>
> - Which 다음에는 명사가 온다. 대답은 I like ~ best.로 하면 된다.
>   Which book do you like best?   너는 어떤 책을 제일 좋아하니?
>   I like *Diary of a Wimpy Kid* best.   나는 Diary of a Wimpy Kid를 제일 좋아해.

Actual Test 2. Bingo with the Amusement Park Ticket

Kevin : Hello, my name is Kevin. And these are my friends Chris and Julie.
Today, we are going to the amusement park.
There are many exciting rides in the amusement park, and we need to complete the bingo with the ticket.
Julie : Hi ~ I'm Julie. I am going to the amusement park with you.
Chris : Hi ~ I'm Chris. I am also completing the bingo with you.

Kevin : 안녕, 나는 케빈이야. 그리고 이쪽은 나의 친구인 크리스와 줄리야.
오늘 우리는 놀이공원에 갈 거야. 놀이공원에는 신나는 놀이기구들이 많이 있고 우리는 티켓 빙고를 완성해야 해.
Julie : 안녕~ 난 줄리야. 너와 함께 놀이공원에 갈 거야.
Chris : 안녕~ 난 크리스야. 나도 너와 함께 빙고를 완성할 거야.

Question 1
p. 125

> **Your Turn!** (Sample Answer)
> I like riding the Ferris wheel.

Kevin : We are going to the amusement park.
There are many exciting rides in the amusement park.
I like roller coasters. It's scary but very fun.
What do you like about the amusement park?
We are going to have fun today! We need to buy tickets first.

Kevin : 우리는 놀이공원에 간다. 놀이공원에는 신나는 놀이기구들이 많이 있어.
나는 롤러코스터를 좋아해. 무섭지만 아주 재미있어. 너는 놀이공원의 어떤 점을 좋아하니?
우리는 오늘 즐거운 시간을 보낼 거야.! 우선 티켓을 사야 해.

Question 2
p. 126

> **Your Turn!** (Sample Answer)
> How much does the ticket cost?
> What souvenirs can we get?
> How many rides are there?

Kevin : We bought tickets! If we complete the bingo on the ticket, we can get some souvenirs.
We can go on many rides and even buy ice cream.
I wonder how many rides I can ride.
What do you want to know about the ticket? Tell me three questions you have about the ticket.
Those are good questions.

Kevin : 티켓을 샀어! 티켓에 있는 빙고를 완성하면 기념품을 받을 수 있어.
놀이기구도 많이 탈 수 있고 아이스크림을 살 수도 있어. 놀이기구를 몇 개나 탈 수 있는지 궁금해.
너는 티켓에 대해 무엇을 알고 싶니? 네가 티켓에 대해 알고 싶은 세 가지 질문을 해 봐.
좋은 질문이야.

[해설]

How much does ~ cost? ~은 얼마예요?

- 가격이나 비용을 물을 때 사용하는 표현으로 does 다음에 물건이나 상품 등이 온다.
  How much does the bike cost? 그 자전거는 얼마예요?
  How much does it cost? 그것은 얼마예요?
- 같은 표현으로 How much is it?을 쓸 수 있다.

Question 3

p. 127

> **Your Turn!** (Sample Answer)
> First, the train has wings. And the driver of the train is a rhinoceros. He is waving. An elephant with balloons is in the nest. There is a boy sleeping.

Kevin : We will take an animal train to get to the gate.
First, these words can help you. I will say a word or a sentence and then you can say it to practice.
nest, wings, wave
Chris : Some strange things are in the train.
For example, the animal train has wings.
Many strange things are in the train.
Kevin : That is strange. Look at the animal train again.
Tell me what is strange. Tell me everything that is strange.
Wow! It is a strange train. Let's take another train.

Kevin : 출입구까지 가기 위해 동물기차를 탈 거야.
먼저, 이 단어들이 도움이 될 거야. 내가 단어나 문장을 말한 후에 네가 연습삼아 따라 말하면 돼. / 둥지, 날개, 흔들다
Chris : 기차에 이상한 것들이 있어.
예를 들면, 동물 기차에 날개가 있어. 기차에 이상한 것들이 많이 있어.
Kevin : 이상하네. 동물 기차를 다시 한 번 봐.
이상한 것을 얘기해줘. 이상한 것을 모두 말해줘.
와! 이상한 기차네. 다른 기차를 타자.

Question 4

p. 128~129

> **Your Turn!** (Sample Answer)
> Julie and Kevin waited on the platform. An animal train arrived. They got on the train and gave their tickets to the rabbit station staff. The rabbit station staff gave them a stamp. Julie fastened a seatbelt. The rabbit station staff sang and drove the train. They got to the amusement park, so they got off the train.

Julie : It's time to take the animal train to get to the amusement park. But first, these words can help you. I will say a word or a sentence and then you can say it to practice.
train station, ticket, wear.
Let's take the animal train. Watch again.
Chris : I didn't see what happened. Tell me what happened.
Tell me everything that happened.
Thank you.

Julie : 놀이공원에 도착하기 위해 동물 기차를 타야 할 시간이야.
그런데 먼저, 이 단어들이 도움이 될 거야. 내가 단어나 문장을 말한 후에 네가 연습삼아 따라 말하면 돼. / 기차역, 티켓, 착용하다.
동물 기차를 타자. 다시 한 번 봐.
Chris : 무슨 일이 벌어졌는지 못 봤어. 무슨 일이 벌어졌는지 말해 봐.
무슨 일이 생겼는지 전부 말해 줘.
고마워.

Question 5

p. 130

> **Your Turn!** (Sample Answer)
> First, wait in line for the Ferris wheel. Next, give the person your ticket. Then ride the Ferris wheel. Finally, get off the Ferris wheel and take your ticket back.

Kevin : We are at the amusement park now!
There are many exciting rides here.
Let me show you how to ride the Ferris wheel.
This word can help you. Ferris wheel. Watch what I do.
Julie : I want to ride the Ferris wheel. But I didn't see how to ride it.
Tell me how to ride the Ferris wheel.
Tell me everything I need to do.
Great! Thank you.

Kevin : 우리는 지금 놀이공원에 와 있어! 여기 신나는 놀이기구들이 많아.
Ferris wheel을 타는 방법을 보여 줄게. 이 단어가 도움이 될 거야. 대회전 관람차. 내가 하는 것을 봐.
Julie : 나는 Ferris wheel을 타고 싶어. 하지만 타는 방법을 보지 못 했어.
Ferris wheel을 타는 방법을 말해 줘. 내가 무엇을 해야 하는지 전부 말해 줘.
좋아! 고마워.

Question 6
p. 131

> **Your Turn!** (Sample Answer)
> Can we go and see the magic show?

Kevin : I think the magic show will be very interesting.
Let's go to see the magic show.
Ask Julie and Chris if we can go to see the magic show.

Julie&Chris : Sure! Let's go to see the magic show.

Kevin : 마술 쇼가 아주 흥미로울 거 같아. 마술 쇼를 보러 가자. 마술 쇼를 보러가도 되는지 줄리와 크리스에게 물어봐.

Julie&Chris : 물론이지! 마술 쇼 보러 가자.

Question 7
p. 132~133

> **Your Turn!** (Sample Answer)
> First, people were sitting and waiting for the magic show. Max was dressed like a wizard. He went on the stage and smiled. He touched the hat with the magic wand. The rabbit engineer came out of the hat. They were holding hands.

Kevin : These words can help you. I will say a word or a sentence and then you can say it to practice.
stage, magic wand, hold hands
Watch what happens at the magic show. Watch again.
What happened at the magic show? What did Max do?
Tell me what Max did.
Thank you.

Kevin : 이 단어들이 도움이 될 거야. 내가 단어나 문장을 말한 후에 네가 연습 삼아 따라 말하면 돼. / 무대, 마술 지팡이, 손을 잡다
마술 쇼에서 무슨 일이 벌어지는지 지켜봐. 다시 한 번 봐.
마술 쇼에서 무슨 일이 벌어졌니? 맥스가 무엇을 했니? 맥스가 무슨 일을 했는지 말해 줘.
고마워.

Question 8
p. 134

> **Your Turn!** (Sample Answer)
> I liked the magic show best because the magic was cool, and the monkey was funny.

Kevin : We had a lot of fun at the amusement park today. It was great!
What did you like best in the amusement park?

Julie : I liked the magic show. It was really funny, and Max was so cute.

Kevin : Look at the pictures.
What did you like best in the amusement park and why?

Julie : It was fun going to the amusement park with you.
Goodbye!

Kevin : 오늘 우리는 놀이공원에서 아주 즐거운 시간을 보냈어. 정말 좋았어!
너는 놀이공원에서 무엇이 가장 좋았어?

Julie : 나는 마술 쇼가 좋았어. 정말 웃겼고, 맥스는 아주 귀여웠어.

Kevin : 그림을 봐. 놀이공원에서 가장 좋았던 것은 무엇이었고, 이유는?

Julie : 너와 함께 놀이공원에 가서 재미있었어.
안녕!

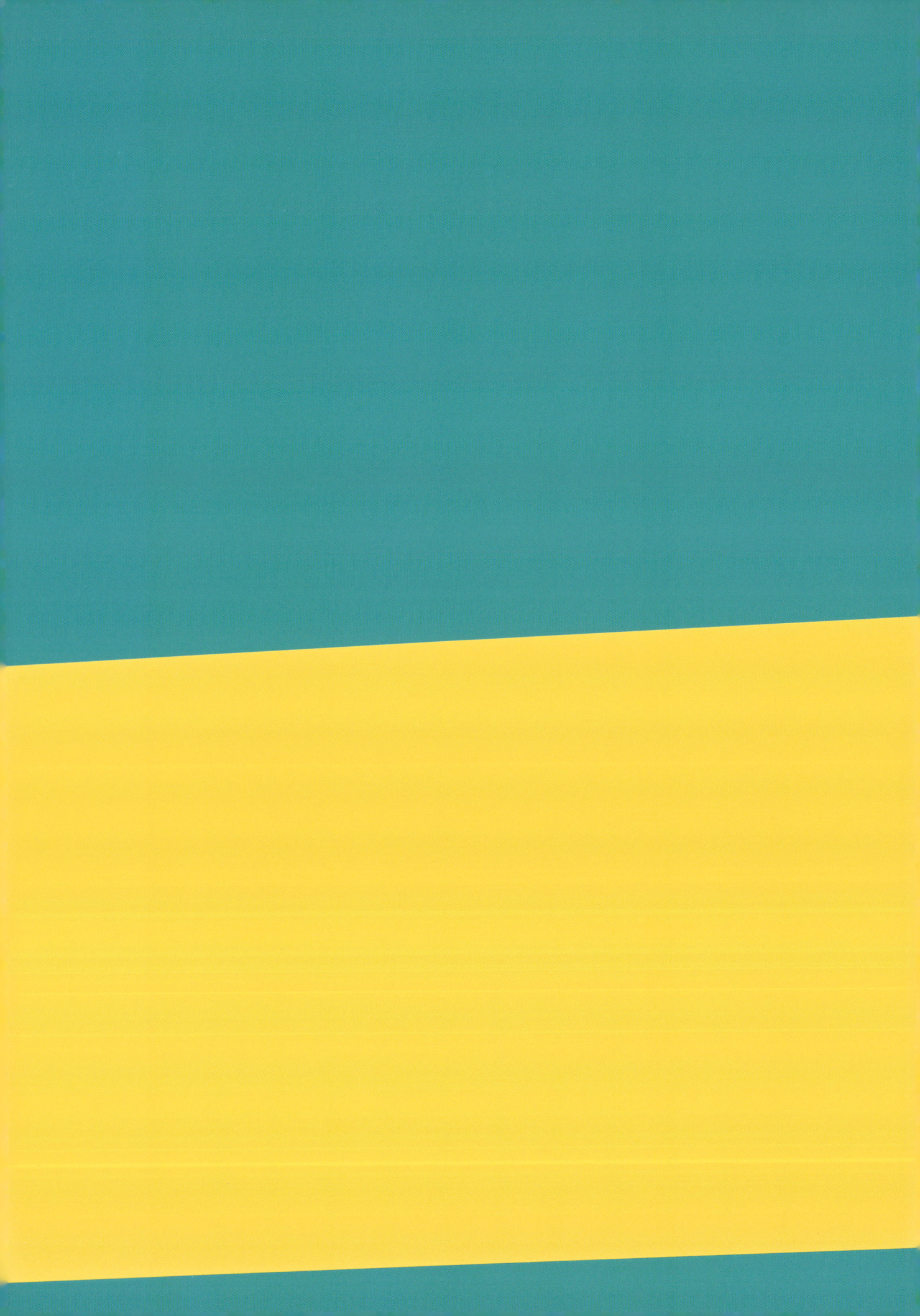